# 100 PURE

# THOUGHTS

# 100 PURE
# THOUGHTS

## Cultivating Purity
## One Thought at a Time

## JOE KIRBY
Off the Kirb Ministries

**CLC**
**PUBLICATIONS**

Fort Washington, PA 19034

*100 Pure Thoughts*

Published by CLC Publications

***USA:*** P.O. Box 1449, Fort Washington, PA 19034
www.clcpublications.com

***UK:*** Kingsway CLC Trust
Unit 5, Glendale Avenue, Sandycroft, Flintshire, CH5 2QP
www.equippingthechurch.com

Printed in the United States of America

ISBN-13 (paperback): 978-1-61958-346-7
ISBN-13 (e-book): 978-1-61958-347-4

Unless otherwise noted, Scripture quotations are from the New King James Version®. Copyright © 1982 by Thomas Nelson. Used by permission. All rights reserved.

Scripture quotations marked NIV are taken from the HOLY BIBLE, NEW INTERNATIONAL VERSION®. NIV®. Copyright © 1973, 1978, 1984 by International Bible Society. Used by permission of Zondervan. All rights reserved worldwide.

Italics in Scripture quotations are the emphasis of the author.

# Acknowledgements

I am very grateful to Dan Balow for prompting me to write this book. His publishing guidance and advice has made my experience as a first-time author very enjoyable.

A special thanks also to Helen Gray for copy editing and ironing out all of my grammatical errors.

Lastly, thank you to my wife, Emma, for marrying an impure man and helping him to fix his eyes on the things of God rather than the things of this world.

# Introduction

If you ask any preacher privately, they'll tell you, "Nobody wants to be the purity guy." It's true—nobody wants to be that guy, because the subject of sexual sin is embarrassing. I used to blush (well, really, *cringe*) whenever a preacher would mention lust in a sermon, but here I am in 2022, writing a book about lust when I wouldn't call myself a "purity preacher," and I certainly wouldn't call myself a writer!

However, two years ago during the first COVID-19 lockdown I received literally thousands of messages through social media from Christians overwhelmed with guilt because of this sin. Many struggled with watching pornography before the pandemic, but when they were confined indoors 24/7 with nothing but a screen to keep them company, they found their addiction snowballed into a monster they simply could not defeat.

But it wasn't just those who struggled with impure images on the Internet who wrote to me; I received messages from those who were having sex outside of marriage, or carrying shame from things they did in a past relationship.

Now you're probably wondering, *Why did all these people write to you Joe? Are you a relationship coach? Do you have a degree in overcoming addictions and psychology?* Far from it! I'm no expert, but in April 2020 I made a very amateur video in my parent's back garden where I shared the most important lesson God ever taught me: *Even though we mess up, He won't stop loving us*. In the Lord's grace the video went viral and has since reached 1.9 million precious souls. Today, in April 2022, men and women, Christian and non-Christian, still message me with the same question: *How do I overcome sexual sin?*

This book is a less-than-perfect answer to that question, from a less-than-perfect man. But my prayer is that this compilation of thoughts which I've picked up over the years will help you. And if just one person breaks free from the chains of lust after reading this book, I will count myself a very blessed man indeed.

# 100 Pure Thoughts

# Thought 1—Admit You've Got a Problem

*If we say that we have no sin, we deceive
ourselves, and the truth is not in us.*

First John 1:8

In every drug and alcohol rehabilitation center they say the first step to freedom is to admit you've got a problem. Sexual sin is no different. The world may say it's natural, your friends may claim your habit isn't as bad as theirs, and even you might not think it's such a big deal. After all, why did God give me such strong desires if He didn't expect me to act on them?

But the Bible says we are not to deceive ourselves: sexual sin is wrong and you need to take action against it. The fact that you have picked up this book is an encouraging sign that you are finally ready to let go of this habitual sin. The verse above reminds us that God knows we're not perfect; we're messy, imperfect sinners who need the Lord's grace daily.

When I first became a Christian I was young and had little money. One day the man who discipled me wanted to buy me a burger at McDonald's, but being British, I felt guilty and stubbornly said, "It's OK; I'm not that hungry, anyway."

He left me smiling and speechless when he responded, "Joe, you can't be a Christian then."

I replied, "What do you mean?"

He laughed. "To be a Christian you need to learn to receive." So I happily let him buy me a Big Mac.

We need to remember the only way we can fight this battle is to accept we're spiritually bankrupt in this area and we need help from the Lord. I pray this book will be used by the Lord to give you the help you need, as we walk this daily journey of purity together.

## Thought 2—No More "Little" Sins

*See now, this city is near enough to flee to,*
*and it is a little one; please let me escape there*
*(is it not a little one?) and my soul shall live.*

Genesis 19:20

You know the story well. God's angels urge Lot and his family to flee from Sodom and Gomorrah because the Lord is going to destroy the city with fire and brimstone—but what does Lot do? He lingers. He stays in Sin City, until the angels must physically drag him and his family out of danger, warning him to run to the mountains for safety. In order to escape the coming judgment, the angels urge Lot to get himself and his family up to the mountains—up, out of, and away from the danger zone. But Lot suggests a compromise. Instead of running a million miles away from Sodom he reasons, *Why can't we go and settle in that tiny, little, harmless city called Zoar? It's only a stone's throw away from where we used to live, and after all, no one likes change.*

It's easy to be comfortable in sin, isn't it? Our lifestyle for years has revolved around this besetting sin. Just as Lot was so attached to Sodom, our habits, routines, and affections might be attached to a place, a situation, or even a person. And yet instead of totally denouncing sin and getting as far away from the evil that God hates, we trade on the mercy of the Lord and say, "Is it really that bad?"

I don't know what compromise looks like in your life. Perhaps social media is the gateway drug into your Internet addiction. Perhaps some of your friends lead you into sin, or maybe there's a place you know that is just plain bad for your soul. Whatever the "little one" is in your life, don't hang around it any longer. Obey God and run to the mountain.

## Thought 3—Chasing More

*Hell and Destruction are never full;*
*So the eyes of man are never satisfied.*

Proverbs 27:20

This verse is one of my favorite verses in the whole Bible. I have memorized it, and it has saved me from so much sin that I recommend you memorize it, too!

King Solomon had everything: twelve thousand horses (the equivalent of sports cars in those days), seven hundred wives and three hundred concubines, masses of gold and a huge empire where he reigned as a powerful and wise king. Solomon had all that the world could ever offer. Everything our culture encourages us to chase after, he had in abundance—and yet, was he happy? No.

In this proverb Solomon was saying that just like hell and the grave will always crave more bodies, so the eyes of man will always crave more. I remember once listening to a very crude comedian before I became a Christian. What he said in that gig has never left me. He said that for hours he would search the Internet trying to find the perfect woman to satisfy his lust. But he never did. Sadly, some of us can relate to that comedian. We know only too well how we have spent hours looking at wrong images thinking we'll find lasting beauty and satisfaction. But we never do. This beauty only exists in the corridors of our mind and the more we chase it, the more disillusioned we become. So today when the Devil whispers in your ear, "If you just have this, you'll be happy," remind yourself that there is only one look that will satisfy the eyes of man and that is to look on the beauty of the Lord.

## Thought 4—Make the Devil Run

*Therefore submit to God. Resist the devil and he will flee from you.*

James 4:7

Every problem the human race has ever faced is because of the first four words in the verse above. Man hates submitting to God. Why do we keep returning to the same sin over and over again? Because our hearts refuse to submit to God's authority. We want to be our own master. We like steering our own ship, but the truth is, the day you hand the wheel to God is the day you find rest. God's power cannot be matched and when we hide behind Jesus we have a new power to resist the Devil.

So let's get practical. What does resisting Satan look like? I'm hoping my wife will never read this book, but let me tell you a secret about my wife. Emma loves chocolate. And in our house you don't have to look hard to find chocolate—next to the fridge there are chocolate eggs, in the freezer is chocolate ice cream, in the family room is chocolate cake, and upstairs in the bedroom there are chocolate bars. And because there was always a plethora of sweet stuff around me, I found myself yielding to the temptation. But here's what's interesting. When I filled the house up with pumpkin seeds, walnuts, vegetables, and tangerines I started eating those things and suddenly I didn't have the same room for those bad, sugary, dopamine hits. It's similar when we submit to God. This means that we should seek to obey His word, read it daily, have fellowship with other Christians, wrestle with Him in prayer daily, and seek to reach the lost every week. If you fill yourself up with those kinds of things, suddenly you will find it much easier to resist the Devil when he dangles a juicy piece of bait in front of your nose.

# Thought 5—The Second Look Is Fatal

*Let your eyes look straight ahead, And your eyelids look right before you.*

Proverbs 4:25

The battle for purity starts on the streets. You can put every accountability system in place to ensure you keep yourself pure in the home, but unless you win the battle on the streets you're already dead in the water.

Sadly, in our society modesty is a long-lost concept and it seems every year outfits for both male and female get more and more provocative. So if we let our eyes wander when we go to the shopping mall, the gym, or even the local park, we will plant seeds of lust that will grow and before you know it you've fallen back into sin again.

Let's grab hold of this advice from the wise old king. When you're walking along the street, when you're out and about seeing people around you, even when you're driving your car and passing by whoever and whatever, keep your gaze forward. Look straight ahead. Remember, the second look is fatal. Imagine a Christian driving past a huge billboard with a sensual image. He can't help that he's seen it, but he has a choice: look straight ahead and keep his eyes pure, or take another look. I believe that when we look again is when it becomes sin. A glance is unavoidable, but a gaze is avoidable. Sounds stressful, right? Well, the Christian life is called a battle for a reason, and in this sex-crazed culture we constantly have to keep looking straight ahead, fixing our eyes on Jesus. It's easy to get distracted by the fleeting pleasures of this world, but we are called to walk by faith and not by sight.

### *Thought 6—Jesus Has Washed Away Your Sins*

*And the blood of Jesus Christ His Son cleanses us from all sin.*

First John 1:7

One day a pastor and a young man were walking down a beach. The young man said to the pastor, "You see these scattered footsteps in the sand? That's what I feel my life has been like. Prone to wander, I've never followed God as I should. Sometimes I doubt I'm even a Christian." As the young man was speaking, a wave came in with a sudden whoosh and wiped away all of the footsteps in the sand. Then the pastor looked at the young man and said, "Yes, but never forget the blood of Jesus Christ washes away all of our sins."

There are times when we lack assurance and our sin makes us feel unworthy to call ourselves Christian. But remember, we are saved by grace. There is no sin that is too vile, too unclean, too bad that the blood of Jesus cannot wash away. The blood that Jesus shed on Calvary scrubs away our sins and makes us whiter than snow. When it snows, the local rubbish heap at the waste collection center looks like Mount Everest. Snow can make all our filthy, rotting material look beautiful because snow covers it with a blanket of perfect spotlessness. In the same way, our sins have been covered by the blood of Jesus Christ. Have you come to Jesus and had your sins washed away? Have you asked Him to be your Lord and Savior? If the answer is no, come to Christ for forgiveness of sins today. If the answer is yes, remind yourself that Christ Jesus came into the world to save sinners. He came not to call the righteous but sinners to repentance.

## *Thought 7—Today You Need to Pray*

*Watch and pray, lest you enter into temptation.*
*The spirit indeed is willing, but the flesh is weak.*

Matthew 26:41

Everyone wants a hack, a silver bullet, a new gimmick, a strategy which will revolutionize their life and defeat this sin once and for all. Imagine we're sitting in a TED talk and the speaker's theme is, "How to be healthy and look after your body." All she would really need to say is, "If you want to be healthy, there are three things you need to do: first, eat healthy; second, exercise daily; and third, get eight hours of sleep every night. OK, that's all from me, bye." Yes, there are nuances, but the bottom line to a healthy lifestyle is diet, exercise, and sleep.

This can be applied to our Christian lives. In very simple terms, if you want to overcome temptation the only solution is prayer, Bible study, and fellowship with other believers. And personally I believe prayer to be the most important! When I used to pray sitting down I found I couldn't concentrate for long. So instead I walk. Sometimes I use the stairs in my house to help me focus, with each new step leading to a new prayer point, but my favorite way to pray is to prayer pace either up and down the garden or during a walk in the quiet of the morning. Some people find praying out loud helps them to concentrate but I find walking is enough to keep focused to do business with God.

One final tip: try using the **A.C.T.S.** acrostic as a checklist for your prayers. Start with **A**doration by praising our amazing God. Then **C**onfession of recent sins you've committed, asking for cleansing from these sins. Next is **T**hanksgiving for the blessings God has given you. And lastly, **S**upplication, making your requests, knowing that He will supply your every need. This method literally changed my prayer life; I hope it changes yours, too!

# Thought 8—Fight with a Sword

*Your word I have hidden in my heart, That I might not sin against You.*

Psalm 119:11

Many Christians want to break free from the chains of lust, but neglect their time alone studying the Word of God. When we do that we put down our sword and try to fight the powers of darkness with a feather. Is it any wonder we are helpless against temptation?

I believe if we knew how powerful the Word of God really was, we would never miss a quiet time. Your daily devotions are like an investment; in the early days you see little profit and it can be very costly. But if you keep investing, eventually you're going to get a big pay day! This can be applied with the Word of God. Every time you read it you plant seeds into the soil of your heart and those seeds will keep growing, until eventually you will see fruit in your life and even the people around you will start to see fruit in your life. So many times the Holy Spirit has brought to my mind an obscure verse that I didn't even know I knew! But because it was hidden in my heart God was able to use it as a secret weapon to keep me from sin. God has given us incredible memories. We can recite songs, phone numbers, and whole movies. But make sure you make the effort to memorize Scripture too, because knowing the lyrics to "Sweet Caroline" won't save you in the battle, but knowing Proverbs 5 will.

## Thought 9—You Cannot Do This Alone

*Not forsaking the assembling of ourselves together, as is
the manner of some, but exhorting one another, and
so much the more as you see the Day approaching.*

Hebrews 10:25

A friend of mine recently commented, "I think there are more Christians in the world who don't attend a local church than those who do." I was stunned, but he was right. I've lost count of the number of Christians who message me through social media to say they left the local church because it was wicked or had compromised on the teachings of the Bible. But just because we've had one bad meal doesn't mean we should never eat again!

I strongly believe that, instead of *preying on* our pastors, we need to be *praying for* our pastors. When struggling with repetitive sin, you need someone to talk to—and not just anyone, but a man of God who has been providentially placed in your local area by the Lord, who can shepherd your heart towards Christ. Fellowship with God must never become singular or self-centered, and I fear too many Christians have become lone rangers. Martyn Lloyd-Jones once said, "My experience in the ministry has been those who are least frequent in their church attendance are also those who are most plagued with problems in life."[1] Just being at church changes our attitude. At church we see those who are going through greater storms than we are, yet have a peace that surpasses all understanding.

We can all agree on one thing: Jesus calls us to serve one another and I cannot see a better vehicle for service, for using your gifts, and for dying to self than in the local church. So stop fighting this battle alone and enlist at your local military station—aka, the church—today.

### *Thought 10—Our Greatest Motivation*

*Blessed are the pure in heart, For they shall see God.*

Matthew 5:8

A crucial question that those who are battling sexual sin should ask themselves is, *Why do I want to repent from this sin?* What's my motivation? Is it the fear of getting caught, of being exposed to my friends and family as a fraud? Is it the fear that God will send me to hell if I do not turn from this sin? Is it the fear that God will chastise me and bring pain into my life because of my disobedience? What's your motive for getting clean?

Our greatest motive should be that the pure in heart will see God. Perhaps I'm the only one who has experienced this, but when I lived a double life, I remember watching wrong things on the Internet and then the next day going on a date with my wife to a place of outstanding beauty, with mountains, lakes, valleys, and wildlife. I'd stand there and know that I should be in awe of God's creation, but my vision was blurred from what I had seen the night before.

Am I the only one who's read powerful Scriptures that should have emotionally moved me, but instead, like a drunken man, my vision was impaired from seeing anything of God? Am I the only one who has walked out of church while the whole congregation is weeping at a movement of God in the service but because my sin has blinded me I saw nothing special?

Rest assured, when the Holy Spirit binds this sin and casts it out of you, you will start to get your vision back; you will see God in ways you've never seen Him before. When this happens you'll see that for such a long time, you traded a chance to gaze on the Lord of Hosts for cheap vulgar images on the Internet. Don't make the same mistake I have; don't waste years looking at filth, but instead fix your eyes upon Jesus.

## Thought 11—The Art of Bouncing

*For a righteous man may fall seven times And rise
again, But the wicked shall fall by calamity.*

Proverbs 24:16

When you received Christ, an invisible target was put on your back; Satan will throw all of hell at you to try to make you fall. The Devil wants to trip you, and he will use whoever and whatever he can to throw you into a ditch. Because we have faith in Jesus we are declared righteous by God, but that doesn't mean we're perfect. God will be continually transforming, shaping, and molding us until the day we die.

I don't have to tell you that Christians fall; this book wouldn't be in your hand if that were not the case. But the Christian life is not about how fast you can run, it's not about how high you can climb—it's about how well you bounce.

The important thing is not what made you fall; neither is it the amount of times you have fallen. The important thing is that when you fall, you rise again. When my son first learned to walk, it was a frustrtating experience. He took two steps, then fell; he got back up and took three steps, then fell; he took four steps, then fell. He repeated this 100 times, maybe 500 times, until eventually . . . what do you think happened? He learned to walk without falling! That's my prayer for you and me—that we learn to walk the Christian life without falling. But if we do fall, don't stay down, don't think God has given up on you. Look up and you'll see the risen Lord Jesus holding his hand out, ready to lift you back on your feet again.

## *Thought 12—Entertainment Won't Set You Free*

*Let our master now command your servants, who are before you,
to seek out a man who is a skillful player on the harp. And it
shall be that he will play it with his hand when the distressing
spirit from God is upon you, and you shall be well.*

First Samuel 16:16

Remember when Saul lost the anointing of God and an evil
spirit began to torment him? It's interesting that Saul didn't
call for Samuel to come and minister to him. He chose musical
entertainment rather than the man of God to deal with the spirit.
In God's grace the Lord providentially sent another man of God,
the soon-to-be king of Israel, David.

Do you see an image of Saul in your own heart? When struggling with strongholds and stress, it's easy to turn to entertainment to soothe us and help us escape the problem, without facing
the real issue head on. Leonard Ravenhill said, "Entertainment is
the devil's substitute for joy. The more joy you have in the Lord,
the less entertainment you need."[2] Jesus said, "Come to Me,
all you who labor and are heavy laden, and I will give you rest"
(Matt. 11:28). But we go to Netflix, Instagram, or music for rest,
even though we know it only covers up the issue.

So let me leave you with two thoughts. First, if there is a
Samuel near you—a pastor or an elder of a local church—make
sure you confide in them about your secret battle. There's nothing
they haven't heard before, no matter how "holy" they look!

Second, be careful how much time you spend with entertainment. Why not swap that TV show for a Christian book, or that
chart topper for a worship song, or even social media for a sermon? You'll be amazed how much more rest you will find when
you start living the radical Christian life.

## Thought 13—Innocent Flirting?

*Do not lust after her beauty in your heart,*
*Nor let her allure you with her eyelids.*

Proverbs 6:25

Do you think there is such a thing as innocent flirting? Personally, I don't. Solomon here describes a woman who catches the attention of men by fluttering her eyelids. Extended eyelashes, sensual clothing, seductive body language—we all know the type of woman that Solomon is warning against. But men can also be like the proverbial peacock, dancing their tail feathers to gain the attention of women.

Beware of flirtation. It's dangerous, because it gives the impression to the other person that they are attractive to you and the heart, which is so delicate, begins to open up and feel tender feelings towards the flirtatious person. Every affair began with "innocent flirting," but because everything in life grows, that flirting grew into adultery. As a Christian you want to stay pure for Jesus, but the person at your work, university or gym probably doesn't see sex as that big a deal. Some view it as no more valuable than eating dinner, so beware of how quickly flirting can turn into something much more sinful. It might seem impossible in the culture we live, but one man managed a greater feat. The evangelist Billy Graham vowed never to be alone with a woman who was not his wife. Some may consider that over the top, but in an era when many famous preachers were involved in scandals, to this day Billy Graham's name has stayed pure, to the credit of our Savior, Jesus Christ.

## Thought 14—Deep Waters

*Your oarsmen brought you into many waters.*

Ezekiel 27:26

Have you ever experienced the aftermath of sin? Sinners may go unpunished for many a bright hour, but mark my words, one day the storm is coming. We can choose the sin, but we can't choose the consequence, and sin never pays its servants a fair wage. Some men are paralyzed by the harvest of their sin twenty years after the seed was sown. They think their sins were like dead men, out of sight, out of mind—but these dead men have been resurrected and have come back to haunt them. At the time the sin seemed pleasant and harmless but now their past has caught up with them. Charles Spurgeon said, "Many a man bears in his bones the sins of his youth."[3]

If you have not experienced the repercussions of your sin, do not hang around to see if God's Word is true. The way of the sinner is hard, but the fear of the Lord leads to life, and there is hope for all of us. You may have rowed into strong waters but only one Man can row you out of them—the Man who the wind and the waves obeyed, the Man who walked on water, the Man who gives us the quenching water of everlasting life: God incarnate, Jesus Christ. Only He can deliver you from these tempestuous seas. So get into His lifeboat today. Though the storm may rage and you may bear the consequences of your sin today, if you've got a Lifeguard who walks on water in your boat—you're eternally safe.

Jesus, lover of my soul, Let me to Thy bosom fly,
While the nearer waters roll, While the tempest still is high:
Hide me, O my Saviour, hide, Till the storm of life is past;
Safe into the haven guide; O receive my soul at last.[4]

## *Thought 15—Above and Beyond*

*And so it was, when those bearing the ark of the LORD*
*had gone six paces, that he sacrificed oxen and fatted sheep.*

Second Samuel 6:13

This is a well-known passage where a man called Uzzah—which means "strong"—was struck down by the Lord for putting his hands on the ark to keep it steady. The Lord wanted the ark to be carried on the shoulders by Levite priests but the men of Israel chose a more "efficient" method, a superior method guided by Mr. Strong, who was not a Levite. So when David went to collect the ark a second time and bring it into Jerusalem he came with humility and was meticulous not to get it wrong again. Some commentators believe that David literally stopped every six steps to offer a sacrifice to the Lord. Suppose they're right—what does that mean? It means David was willing to go above and beyond to live consecrated to the Lord. He was not commanded to stop every six steps but he did it to make sure he killed the flesh. Your other Christian friends may be content to watch unclean movies, to listen to ungodly music, to stay up late and live out a comfortable Christianity. But if you want to reach another level, you've got to go to the next level of sacrifice like David. Discipline equals freedom. Yes, it might be inefficient; yes, people will think you're crazy; but instead of being led by the flesh (which, by the way, is represented in the Bible as the number six) we need to stop, keep short accounts all day, and keep coming back to God in confession and prayer. For without Him we can do nothing.

## Thought 16—I Caught a Thought

*Casting down arguments and every high thing*
*that exalts itself against the knowledge of God, bringing*
*every thought into captivity to the obedience of Christ.*

Second Corinthians 10:5

Catching thoughts is much harder than it sounds. Martin Luther famously said, "You cannot keep birds from flying over your head but you can keep them from building a nest in your hair."[5] You may not realize it, but your mind is full of philosophies, strongholds, arguments, and ideas that try to steal the throne of your heart from Christ. Ever since we were children we have drunk in the world's belief systems; they have contaminated our minds more than we would like to admit.

Hands down, the worst period of my life was when I had a sort of mid-life crisis at the age of twenty-five. I had been listening to various social media influencers who had taught me life was essentially like an orange and I needed to squeeze every last drop of juice out of it before I die. Without going into details, it took me down a dark path of rebellion against God.

This would never have happened if when I first heard these ideas I had taken the thoughts captive. Every thought must bow to God. Pluck out those evil thoughts before they take root; if you let them stay overnight they will be deep-rooted in the morning.

Everything must be surrendered to Jesus: our time, bodies, money, house, and family must all be wedded to God. When I was thirteen I used to wear a plastic wrist band with the initials W.W.J.D.—you all know what it stands for: "What Would Jesus Do?" It was great because all day long I had the constant reminder that I was to act like how Jesus acted. Well, perhaps someone should bring the bands back into fashion but make one with these initials W.W.J.T.—"What Would Jesus *Think*?"

## Thought 17—No More Empty Promises

*I have made a covenant with my eyes;*
*Why then should I look upon a young woman?*

Job 31:1

Job begins his speech of why his sufferings are not due to his sin by starting with a tremendous covenant. Somewhere Job made a whole-hearted decision that he would never gaze at a young woman (or virgin as described in other translations).

When the prophet Daniel resolved that he would not defile himself with the king's food, he made a serious set-in-stone decision not to be unclean.

So what about you, then?

Have you burned your boats and made a solemn decision that you will never sail across to Sin Island again?

We will never find victory until our whole heart is in this decision to be pure. You've made empty promises in the past before. But God does business only with those who mean business.

The stoat, or short-tailed weasel, has such a pure silky coat that for centuries it has been a symbol for purity. The stoat takes pride in its pure coat and will do anything it can to keep it clean. Hunters know their prey's weakness and exploit it by smearing filthy grime around the entrance hole of the stoat's burrow. As the hunting dogs chase down their prey, the stoat runs to its burrow for cover. However, when it sees the vile filth at the entrance to its home, rather than defiling its perfectly white coat it turns around and faces the dogs instead. In other words, it would rather die than defile itself.

The day that you and I become that desperate for purity will be the day we find it.

## Thought 18—Protect Your Portals

*I will set nothing wicked before my eyes.*

Psalm 101:3

The raw truth is this: you have a problem with purity today because you have set wicked things before your eyes in the past. Our eyes are the gates to the rest of our body, they are the portals to the soul and whatever fascinates your eyes will soon gain admission to the heart. If you want to defeat the sin of lust, there is no other option but to learn how to control your eyes. The Devil is crafty; he shows you just enough to intrigue you and then he increases the temptation with every look. Each piece of bait gets larger and more irresistible until we find ourselves captured by a cold, cruel hook and realize we've been click-baited yet again.

So don't fall for the bait; aimless scrolling on your phone is inviting disaster. Watching wicked things on TV will not do, either. If we are vigilant in the early stages with what things we watch and what games we play, it will be much easier to nip the sin in the bud before it gets bigger. So today when your eyes lock onto something enticing, remember it always leaves you empty. Sin always overpromises. If a castle only has one weak spot, one possible access point for the enemy to invade, you know the king's soldiers will do all they can to defend this single entry point. Shouldn't we also do all we can to defend our only access point, by protecting our eyes against the armies of lust?

## Thought 19—Don't Feed the Bad Wolf

*That you put off, concerning your former conduct, the old man
which grows corrupt according to the deceitful lusts, and be renewed
in the spirit of your mind, and that you put on the new man which
was created according to God, in true righteousness and holiness.*

Ephesians 4:22–24

Admittedly, I'm terrible at manual labor, but when I do at-
tempt it, it's not long before my clothes stink with sweat
and dirt. So I climb into the shower to get clean, enjoy the
sweet-smelling aromas of shampoo and soap, and dry myself off
with a towel, only to find I have no clean clothes. So I have no
choice but to put my old, sweaty, grimy clothes back on. That's
the picture here in Ephesians 4. If we are trusting in Christ, we
have been washed clean by His blood, yet in our foolishness we
run back to the filth and put on our dirty clothes.

So the question needs to be asked: how do we put on the new
man and kill the old man in us? This old Cherokee proverb[6] should
shed some light. One day an elderly grandfather sat down with
his grandson to teach him all about life. He said to his grandson,
"There is a fight going on inside me. It's a fight between two wolves.
One wolf is evil—he is anger, lust, pride; he is full of greed, tells
many lies, is very jealous, and has a big ego. But the other wolf is
good—he is love, joy, peace; he is full of hope, generosity, humility,
and faith." Then he looked at his grandson and he said, "The same
fight that is in me is going on inside every human being, and I'll tell
you something else, boy—it's going on inside you, too." The grandson was a little shaken up and nervously asked, "So Grandfather,
which wolf will win, then?" The grandfather smiled and whispered
back, "The one you feed." Let us feed the spirit that yearns for
Christ and starve that old wolf that obeys the flesh.

## Thought 20—Know Your Enemy

*Be sober, be vigilant; because your adversary the devil walks about like a roaring lion, seeking whom he may devour.*

First Peter 5:8

Sometimes the Devil sneaks up on us craftily and silent like a snake. As the Puritan once said, "Satan rocks the cradle when we sleep at our devotions."[7] But at other times the Evil One takes another form like a lion and will boldly roar in our faces to try to terrify us. Lions are unpredictable and may attack suddenly for no reason; likewise the Devil will roar a temptation in our face when we are least expecting it. Know your enemy! A huge mistake we make in modern-day Christianity is to spell devil with a small "d." The Devil is a real person, and when you realize you are dealing with an intelligent adversary, you take your Christian battle more seriously. This lion is prowling around day after day with his pride of demons, looking for Christians to rip to pieces.

The Devil shows no mercy. He wants to devour you; he never gives you a day off and will assault you day after day with the same temptation, but you must resist him. If you spot the lion in the distance, you have a much better chance of escaping than if he pounces on you while you are asleep. That's why we as believers must be alert!

I enjoy daily morning prayer walks in the fields near my house. In the springtime the local farmer puts some young bulls in the field, too. I'm no farmer, but it's my understanding they are too young to attack or be aggressive—but that doesn't stop me looking over my shoulder and keeping a close eye on them as I'm walking through the fields. (I've seen them run, and if they charged at me, I'd be finished!) We must also be vigilant and look over our shoulder because I can assure you of one thing—if the Devil was a bull he wouldn't think twice about charging at us!

29

# Thought 21—Remember, You Are Righteous

*For as by one man's disobedience many were made sinners,*
*so also by one Man's obedience many will be made righteous.*

Romans 5:19

Sometimes I think as Christians we lose battles because we forget who we are in Christ. But the glorious truth of the Bible is, if we have been born again we are declared righteous!

Think of it as three transfers from three bank accounts: Adam's bank, your bank, and Jesus' bank. Adam's bank account is full of debt. When he disobeyed God, mankind was cursed, hopelessly in debt to the living God for their disobedience and unable to escape death, the results of this debt.

The first transfer is a hopeless debt—our bankrupt ancestor, Adam, transfers his debt into our account. We are all born into spiritual debt and stained by sin, just like Adam. But when Jesus died on the cross, He took the sins of the world in His body and endured the wrath of God as a punishment for our sins.

That's the second transfer: our debt was accredited into Christ's account and He paid for it in full. So the worst of us is imputed onto Jesus Christ. But here's the crazy part: the best of Jesus Christ is accredited into our account!

That's the third transfer—sometimes called the great exchange. Christ takes the judgment of God for our sins and clothes us in His righteousness. So any repentant sinner who asks Jesus to save them isn't seen as an impure, lustful, lying, wretched sinner anymore, but is clothed in the beauties of Christ.

That's why it's called the "gospel"—because it's *good news*!

## Thought 22—You've Got a New Boss

*For you, brethren, have been called to liberty;*
*only do not use liberty as an opportunity for*
*the flesh, but through love serve one another.*

Galatians 5:13

Picture yourself working in a busy coffee shop with two managers. The first manager is aggressive, arrogant, and self-seeking, but the second, the new manager, is kind, gentle, and loving, but he will fight to protect his employees. Every day the two managers clash over the way the staff should be treated. Whoever wins the fight is the boss of the coffee shop—at least for ten minutes or so, until the other manager gets back up and fights for their opportunity to rule.

This is how many people wrongly view the Christian life. They see the flesh as too strong for the Holy Spirit to overcome, so a constant battle ensues over who will rule the Christian's life that day. But the Bible teaches us the old man Adam has been defeated and now Christ reigns over the believer.

Yes, some days the coffee-shop workers may forget who their boss is and return to their old manager's systems and habits, because it's what they've been used to for so many years. But the true believer has a new character, radically changed by the indwelling Holy Spirit. So never forget, you have been called to freedom—live like a free person today!

## Thought 23—Fruit Inspection

*But the fruit of the Spirit is love, joy, peace,*
*longsuffering, kindness, goodness, faithfulness,*
*gentleness, self-control. Against such there is no law.*

Galatians 5:22–23

Here's a question to ponder: from the day of your conversion, what fruit you have produced? Do you have more love for the things of God, more peace? Are you able to be longsuffering to those who irritate you? Are you kind? Are you gentle? Do you have self-control over your eyes, your mind, your diet, your sleep patterns?

The evidence that a man or woman has been born from above is that they produce the fruits of the Spirit. Sometimes the fruit is small or unimpressive, but the point is this—a true Christian will always produce fruit. An apple tree will always bear apples and though the apples might be little, they are still apples.

It's vital that every Christian takes the time to examine themselves, to ask hard questions to make sure they are truly in the faith. Though I'm an imperfect sinner, am I growing more like Jesus each day, or have I not really changed since coming to Christ? Would others recognize fruit in my life, or do I live no different from an unbeliever? I remember hearing once that Spurgeon had four tests[8] he did every year to examine himself that he was truly saved. If "the Prince of Preachers," who knew the Bible better than you and I put together, saw the importance of searching his heart and affections, don't you think perhaps we should, too?

# Thought 24—Slow and Steady Wins the Race

*For you were once darkness, but now you are*
*light in the Lord. Walk as children of light.*

Ephesians 5:8

Suppose I was a fitness coach and I turned up at your house right now unannounced and told you to grab your running shoes because we're going to do a marathon, right now. How far do you think you could run? If your fitness is anything like mine perhaps a couple of minutes at best and for the vast majority of the time you would need to walk. Why? Because walking is sustainable, but running is not. All through the Bible is this same picture of the child of God walking.

God doesn't want flash-in-the-pan Christians. Today you may run like Usain Bolt, but what will you do for the Lord tomorrow? God desires us to be steady Christians, not spectacular Christians. What are you like when you're alone? Are you the same person when you're surrounded by believers as you are when surrounded by unbelievers? What's your Christian walk like at 10 a.m. versus 10 p.m.? Like a lazy student in a gym class, it's easy to run and look active when the teacher's eyes are on you. But as Christian people we must be consistent—consistent in our daily devotions, our church attendance, our repentance. Often we want to conquer the world for the Lord—and that's a fantastic goal to have! But the reality is God's Word teaches us to walk, because walking is achievable and ensures that every day we make progress.

## Thought 25—Take Ownership for Your Sin

*Let him who stole steal no longer, but rather let him*
*labor, working with his hands what is good, that*
*he may have something to give him who has need.*

Ephesians 4:28

Imagine a thief enters your church, sits next to you, and complains, "I can't stop breaking into people's houses and stealing things! It's my besetting sin. I keep begging the Lord to take this sin out of my life, but so far nothing has changed. I'm still stealing things."

What would you say to him? I think you'd say, "It's not God's responsibility to stop you from stealing; no, that responsibility is on you. Only you can turn from this sin." It sounds obvious and yet that's how many Christians treat their sexual sin. They keep praying that God would automatically remove it with no effort on their part.

Please don't misunderstand me; I believe in prayer. Pretty much every day I pray that God would keep me pure. But nowhere in the Bible does it say, "If you pray, this sin will magically be erased from your life." After He forgave her, Jesus said to the woman caught in adultery, "Go and sin no more" (John 8:11). So it is your responsibility to stop—to seek accountability, to fast, to pray, to guard, to flee, to be radical. Only you can turn from sexual sin; no one can do it for you. Once I understood this, I really started to see the fruits of true repentance in my life.

# Thought 26—The Unfair Trade-Off

*Now therefore, the sword shall never depart from your*
*house, because you have despised Me, and have taken*
*the wife of Uriah the Hittite to be your wife.*

Second Samuel 12:10

Whenever a preacher preaches on sexual sin, it's hard not to mention David and Bathsheba. You probably know the story well. David was supposed to be out to battle; instead he was gazing on the roof of his palace, and saw a beautiful woman named Bathsheba, bathing. He did his research and brought Bathsheba to the palace so he could lie with her. After he committed adultery, Bathsheba became pregnant. David tried to cover up his tracks by getting Bathsheba's husband Uriah to go into his wife. But Uriah was a loyal military man, more concerned about king and country than his leisure time. David eventually got Uriah off the scene by having him fight on the front line in battle. Uriah was killed in action and David wasted no time taking Bathsheba for himself and marrying her.

This matter displeased the Lord, and He sent the prophet Nathan with a severe message: "The sword shall never depart from your house" (2 Sam. 12:10). The prophecy came true. Four of David's sons died before him. One of his sons, Absalom, seized the kingdom and forced David to go on the run again. Perhaps worst of all, his son Amnon also could not control his lusts and took David's daughter (his half-sister) and raped her.

When you look at the grief David suffered after his affair with Bathsheba, you've got to admit that's a pretty high price to pay for a couple of minutes of passion. Sin never pays a fair wage and the trade-off is always unfair. So when you're tempted today, remember the momentary pleasures of sin will never outweigh the pain that comes later. You can choose the sin, but you can't choose the consequences.

## Thought 27—Lust Kills Things

*Then, when desire has conceived, it gives birth to sin;*
*and sin, when it is full-grown, brings forth death.*

James 1:15

Lust is a strong, passionate, burning desire to have something, a craving of the flesh that produces unrest and desperation. There is no clearer illustration of a lustful man than David's son Amnon (whom we will also study tomorrow).

Amnon had a lustful desire for his half-sister Tamar. It was so strong that some translations state Amnon was "obsessed" to the point it make him ill. Mental illness is a serious problem in our society, but did you know that at least one form of mental illness, known as "spiritual depression," can be triggered by sin? Amnon's lust was eating him alive and making him ill. John Owen said, "Be killing sin or it will be killing you,"[9] and because Amnon did not kill sin in those early stages and flee from youthful lusts, it killed him.

Kill sin before it is fully grown. God in His mercy always gives us a window of opportunity to repent, and we must jump through that window before sin is fully grown. In the biblical account of Amnon's story, Jonadab's manipulative friend came up with a plan to get Tamar and Amnon alone. Amnon faked being sick and asked his father David to send his daughter (Tamar) to feed him. Amnon sent everyone out the room, grabbed Tamar and tried to seduce her. She refused and pleaded with Amnon to stop; she even used wisdom to try to persuade Amnon, showing him that this single act would ruin the rest of his life. But remember this, lust never listens. Love is wise and cares about the person, lust is foolish and only cares about self. If you do not kill lust now, it will kill your marriage or your future marriage because lust revolves around *you*.

## Thought 28—Amnon's Repulsion

*Then Amnon hated her exceedingly, so that the hatred with*
*which he hated her was greater than the love with which*
*he had loved her. And Amnon said to her, "Arise, be gone!"*

Second Samuel 13:15

Our story continues: Amnon ignored the wise rebukes of Tamar, cruelly forced himself on her, and suddenly three things died.

First, the relationship between Amnon and Tamar died. Amnon represents many a young man in the twenty-first century. While most men would never go to the same lengths as Amnon to get what they desire, many men do go to great lengths to get what they want from women.

How many times have you heard of a young guy breaking a girl's heart? How common are the words, "He said he loved me, but when he got what he wanted, he dumped me." Sadly, we live in a world where many men use love to get sex, and many women use sex to get love. It never works that way; that's why sex was designed by God to remain in marriage. The moment Amnon's fantasy became reality, he became angry that it did not deliver what it promised, and he took out his anger on his victim, Tamar.

Sexual sin often converts into anger; that's why a common symptom of a pornography addict is irritability. So here's a warning to the unmarried: if you think that sexual intercourse will take your relationship to the next level, you're wrong. It will kill it, because a relationship founded on lust and not love always dies.

The second thing that died was Amnon's reputation. He was supposed to be the next king; instead, he became a fool. Sadly, women also lose their reputation when they try to win a man over by sleeping with him. He may not kill her physically, but he will kill her with words, such as unkind talk about her body—either to her face or to his friends.

And the last thing to die was Amnon himself—killed by his vengeful brother Absalom. Tamar was left feeling trashed and used. She wandered the palace in ashes, mourning over her precious virginity. But Amnon was killed two years later when he was drunk on wine (still a man lacking self-control) by Absalom's servants. Although we may not be killed physically for our lust, if we refuse to repent from our sin it will lead to the second death: an eternity separated from God.

## Thought 29—Men Love Flattery

*To keep you from the evil woman,*
*from the flattering tongue of a seductress.*

Proverbs 6:24

Many men are craving affirmation, perhaps because they have known rejection for much of their life. Maybe they are demeaned at home on a daily basis by their wife or family. Maybe they are just plain insecure. Whatever the reason, many men are desperate to hear something positive about themselves.

That's where the seductress, or "strange woman" in the KJV, comes in. She is a strange woman, not in the sense of being odd, but not being his wife. She is outside his family—a stranger to him.

She comes in all forms. She may be a coworker who says, "You're so creative," or the barista at Starbucks who is overly friendly. She might be your neighbor who laughs loudly at your unfunny jokes.

To any woman reading this, let me say two things. First, though this verse applies to men, everything I've said can also apply to you. Women also crave love and acceptance that they might not get from their husband. The second thing I'd like to gently say to you is, if you're married, make sure you encourage your husband. He may seem tough on the outside, but all husbands need a loving wife to build them up. Sadly, some men do feel like total losers, and if they don't get attention from any of the people mentioned above, where do they go? Pornography.

Much of the unclean websites men watch are centered on giving a man a false sense of feeling special, with the actresses saying everything a man is desperate to hear. If that's you, listen to this warning from Solomon: "The stranger . . . flattereth with her words" (Prov. 7:5, KJV). It's all an act and the scriptwriter (Satan) knows just what to say to distract you from the ways of the Lord.

## Thought 30—The Devil Makes Work for Idle Hands

*It happened in the spring of the year, at the time when kings go out to battle, that David sent Joab and his servants with him, and all Israel; and they destroyed the people of Ammon and besieged Rabbah. But David remained at Jerusalem.*

Second Samuel 11:1

The saying is true: "The Devil makes work for idle hands." Here we see King David neglecting his duties as king. He was supposed to be battling; instead he was browsing, wandering aimlessly on the palace roof. As we've already seen, it was here he saw Bathsheba bathing, and his lust for her was ignited. I do believe lust and laziness go hand in hand. Those with no project to work on, no goals to strive for, who stay up all night playing video games and only get up at 10 a.m., are often the same ones who live in habitual sexual sin.

I've noticed in my own life that when I take a day off and just lie awake in bed in the morning, temptations start to enter my mind. When I realize what's happening, I jump up and set my mind to a task—and suddenly the thoughts disappear.

Don't give Satan a foothold. Temptation is inevitable for the believer, but if we live a lazy lifestyle we are inviting a beating from Beelzebub. Apparently, experts tell us that exercising to the point of exhaustion is scientifically proven to help overcome a pornography addiction. That makes sense, because God created our bodies to labor in a field, to be physical and to exert energy. The human body contains sixty thousand miles of blood vessels; that means they could wrap around the earth two-and-a-half times. These blood vessels were designed to work, pumping oxygen through the body.[10] But many of us spend our days sitting at a desk, slumped in a chair. So perhaps a very practical tip for you today is to integrate some serious exercise into your routine. It will keep your mind and body busy; besides, your doctor may thank me for it!

## Thought 31—Good Fathers Discipline Their Children

*For whom the LORD loves He chastens, And scourges every son whom He receives. If you endure chastening, God deals with you as with sons; for what son is there whom a father does not chasten?*

Hebrews 12:6–7

A gifted artist was once asked, "How did you sculpt such a beautiful elephant?" The artist replied, "I just chip away everything that doesn't look like an elephant." We often see God's discipline as a bad thing, as if the God of the universe is some big ogre who loves to wag his finger at us in disapproval. But actually God is a loving Father. He sees the sins that ruin us and in His mercy He chips them away. Both my dad and my grandpa have had skin cancer, and for the surgeon to cut that cancer out of the flesh is a very painful process, but it takes the poison away. Likewise God will chip away at us; perhaps it's our unwillingness to repent from sexual sin, or maybe it's our pride, but be sure of this—if you don't deal with it yourself, God will deal with it and it will hurt. That's why wise believers should do everything in their power to humble themselves, because when the Lord humbles, He *really* humbles.

If right now you are reading this and you are enduring the discipline of the Lord, don't despise it. See it as a mark of love from your heavenly Father. When I take my son to the playground and I see other children misbehaving, I don't start disciplining them because they are not mine. And so the unbeliever down the road may get away with murder, but God brings His heavy hand down upon you for one piece of gossip. Don't be angry. It's a sign that you are a child of God. He will not stop chipping away at our sinful character until He sees Christ, His only begotten Son.

"For whom He foreknew, He also predestined to be conformed to the image of His Son, that He might be the firstborn among many brethren" (Rom. 8:29).

## Thought 32—The World Waxes Worse

*But evil men and impostors will grow worse*
*and worse, deceiving and being deceived.*

Second Timothy 3:13

When I was a boy there was a DVD and VCR shop just a few hundred yards from my house. In the days before Netflix and online movies, the cheapest way to catch a movie was to rent it for a few nights. I remember having friends over for a sleepover and my dad took us to the local DVD shop to let us pick a film for the night. It was always so embarrassing, because movies had ratings according to age: those not for all ages were labeled 12+, 15+ and 18+, and the age ratings were a little lax for my parents' values. Some of the films that my friends were allowed to watch, I wasn't able to because of my Christian upbringing. I remember my friend said once, "Why won't your dad let you watch a 12+? You *are* 12!"

Now, as a dad myself, I'm concerned that there is literally no filtering system for kids these days. TikTok, Instagram, and YouTube are rife with adult content; even small children can access it today. "Entertainment" is getting worse and worse. Satan is so crafty at deceiving young people today. Any child without a smart phone is treated like an alien, so most children have them. That means that from a young age, children's brains are conditioned to watch one-minute videos, to be constantly scrolling and distracted, killing their attention spans so they can't focus on a sermon. Reading has become a thing of the past for many young people; getting a teenager to read the Bible seems nearly impossible. But perhaps worst of all, they have easier access to pornography, in much larger quantities, than earlier generations ever had. My challenge for you today is to pray for a young person in your life, that God would shield them from this wicked world and keep them pure in this modern-day Babylon.

## Thought 33—How to Slay a Giant

*David fastened his sword to his armor and tried to walk, for he had not tested them. And David said to Saul, "I cannot walk with these, for I have not tested them." So David took them off.*

First Samuel 17:39

As a little boy, one of my favorite stories was the battle between David and Goliath. When I got older, I realized it wasn't just a story for children, but one that adults need to ponder, too. As David stepped out in faith, ready to fight the enemy, it's interesting to note how his oldest brother Eliab tried to demoralize him. Often when we seek to live by faith it's our nearest and dearest, those who live with us, who try to discourage us. But in those moments we must keep our eyes fixed on the path God has called us to walk.

It's also interesting that when we face giants, others may try to prescribe to us their method of handling it. Saul thought he'd help by giving David his armor to wear, but David was too small, and the armor didn't fit his frame. There's a lesson for us in this, too. God engineers various methods to help us defeat our giants, and just because it works for someone else doesn't mean it will work for you. God may have a completely different battle plan for you. When David finally squared up to Goliath he killed him with a sling—not much different to what the kids down the street shoot Coke cans with! To quote E.M. Bounds, "The church is looking for better methods, but God is looking for better men."[11]

We often measure everything by what we see or what we hear and it leads us to discouragement. But when we walk by faith, God comes into our lives and does the unexplainable. Right now, you may be facing an even scarier giant than the nine-foot Goliath—the giant of sexual sin. Never let anyone say, "This is the only method," because we're all different and only God knows how to make the giant fall in your life.

*"For all those things My hand has made, And all those things exist,"*
*Says the LORD. "But on this one will I look: On him who is poor*
*and of a contrite spirit, And who trembles at My word."*

Isaiah 66:2

Ever wondered where the Quakers got their name? Well, the outsiders used to observe the Quakers and how they trembled at God's Word. Therefore, as a form of mockery they were named "Quakers." Whether you're part of the denomination or not, there are few men and women today who tremble over the Word of God. We've become so casual about sin, when the reality is the Bible tells us we should be terrified. I am a big believer that we should bask in the grace of God, but if every preacher alive only preaches "grace, grace, grace" it leads to a lack of holiness in the church. Equally, if a preacher only preaches "judgment, judgment, judgment" his congregation either becomes very anxious or very pharisaical. Instead, we need balance in our theology. That's why I'm just asking you this today: *Do you have a contrite spirit? Do you feel your sin and mourn over it, or have you become immune to the warnings of the Scriptures?* If your response isn't positive, pray that God would turn you into a "quaker"—a Christian who is not trivial over the Word, but trembles at the Word.

# Thought 35—Perhaps This Is Why You're Anxious . . .

*The wicked flee when no one pursues,*
*But the righteous are bold as a lion.*

Proverbs 28:1

You've probably heard that people who frequently consume Internet porn are also more prone to depression, loneliness, and anxiety. Even secular psychologists are noticing this strong link in their research. The truth is this sin turns men into cowards. There is nothing worse than the terrors of a guilty conscience. Adam was the first man to flee when no one was pursuing him. "And they heard the sound of the Lord God walking in the garden . . . and Adam and his wife hid themselves from the presence of the Lord God among the trees of the garden" (Gen. 3:8). God was *walking*, He wasn't *stalking*. And Adam hid because he thought God was chasing him.

When I was eleven I stole some shiny hubcaps off a Mini-Cooper parked at a gym near my house. The man caught me and began to chase me from the parking lot. I hopped on my bike, cycled into the woods, and hid, terrified. After the incident, I cut my hair short and started wearing different clothes. Every day for several months I kept looking out the window of my house, afraid that every passing car was that man, bringing the police to arrest me.

I also remember once asking the teacher who gave me detention if it would go on my record for life and keep me from getting a job. (The teacher, spitefully, said yes!) Sin makes us paranoid; I could tell you stories, even as an adult, where I "fled without a cause."

If we have been saved and redeemed by the blood of Christ, we are no longer wicked, but righteous—but that doesn't make us immune from the terrors of sin. So my question to you is, have you considered that perhaps you're so anxious because you are burdened by a guilty conscience? I pray that you will repent of this sin and let the Lord transform you into a bold lion for Him.

## Thought 36—Hiding Sin under the Tent

*And Achan answered Joshua and said, "Indeed I have sinned against the Lord God of Israel, and this is what I have done: When I saw among the spoils a beautiful Babylonian garment, two hundred shekels of silver, and a wedge of gold weighing fifty shekels, I coveted them and took them. And there they are, hidden in the earth in the midst of my tent, with the silver under it."*

Joshua 7:20–21

Are you a public success but a private failure? At the time I'm writing this, we've seen some big names exposed in the Christian world—preachers and evangelists who had perfect "sin systems." They had mastered the art of covering their sin, and had gotten away with deception and immorality for so long that they thought they were untouchable. Sin had lulled them into a false sense of security and taken their raft out into deep waters; just when they thought the water was totally calm, sin ripped off the garment that was covering them to expose their darkness to the rest of the world.

In the Bible we read of Achan—the man who stole from God. After Jericho was conquered by the Israelites, they were commanded to dedicate all of the plunder to the Lord. But Achan saw some silver, some gold, and a fine Babylonian garment, stole them all, and buried them under his tent. Just picture that in your mind's eye: a big bump in the middle of Achan's tent where his secret was hidden. Achan thought that he had tricked everyone but the eyes of the Lord, which are on every place, saw Achan's sin, and brought judgment on Achan and the people of Israel for his private misconduct. Achan was stoned to death. His secret was brought out into the light.

When God looks at the tent of your life, is there a bump of some treasure that you're hiding from the rest of the world? If the answer is yes, what is the sin you're hiding from God? Are you willing to dig it up and destroy it before it destroys you?

# Thought 37—Never Give Up

*And let us not grow weary while doing good, for*
*in due season we shall reap if we do not lose heart.*

Galatians 6:9

In 1968 John Stephen Akhwari was running for his country Tanzania in the Olympics hosted by Mexico City. During the 42-km race he cramped up and collided with other racers. On his fall he dislocated his shoulder and wounded his knee dreadfully. As Akhwari scrambled to get up, he was covered in a mixture of blood, dirt, and sweat. It was obvious that John Stephen Akhwari needed medical attention; surely he would pull out of the race.

But John shocked the world when he started running again— well, actually, he didn't run; he slowly limped, all the way to the finish line. His time: 3:25:27, an hour later than the winner, Mamo Wolde. His spectators: a small crowd—practically everyone had left the stadium. His finishing place: last out of all the fifty-seven competitors who completed the race. When it was all over, a stray interviewer asked John Stephen Akhwari, "Why didn't you quit?" His response was, "My country did not send me 5,000 miles to start the race; they sent me 5,000 miles to finish the race."[12]

Christian, God did not save you to start the race. He saved you so that you might finish the race. I know you may feel like giving up; it's so hard battling for purity. It can feel too hard to follow Jesus—and you're right! Being a Christian is tough, but when you finally cross the finish line and can say like the apostle Paul, "I have fought the good fight, I have finished the race, I have kept the faith" (2 Tim. 4:7–8), it will all be worth it. So dear Christian, whatever you do, don't give up today!

## Thought 38—How Does This End?

*When I thought how to understand this, It was too*
*painful for me—Until I went into the sanctuary*
*of God; Then I understood their end.*

Psalm 73:16–17

When I was younger something attacked my mind and led me into much sexual sin; it's called "FOMO"—the "fear of missing out." I looked at celebrities and social media stars and longed to live a life of luxury and pleasure like they did.

In Psalm 73 Asaph asks a similar question: *Why do the wicked prosper, but the righteous go unrewarded?* So let's deal with this question: *Is being a Christian a waste of time?*

Jack Nicholson has led an enviable life, in the eyes of most men of the world. He is rich, successful, and (so he claims) has slept with over 2,000 women. But people who envy the Jack Nicholsons of the world never ask the question, "How does such a lifestyle end?" People always see the beginning but not the end.

So how has Jack Nicholson's life ended? In a 2014 interview, Nicholson said he regrets his philandering; no woman will ever trust him, so he's "scared of dying in the house on my own."[13]

The death of the ungodly is a terrible thing. Contrast that with the life of the godly which on the surface seems narrow, boring, and a miserable way to spend your life. But the question is, how do we end? Christians go the grave with peace, knowing this is not the end, but the beginning. The foolish prophet Balaam observed this and said, "Let me die the death of the righteous" (Num. 23:10).

Back to the original question: *Is being a Christian a waste of time? Are we missing out?* As every man's life draws to an end who is the one who really prospers—the righteous or the unbeliever?

Just as Asaph had this revelation when he entered into the sanctuary of God, John Wesley came to the same conclusion about the end of the righteous. He said, "Our people die well."[14] The next time you find yourself envious of unbelievers in the world, look to the future and remember: you're on the winning side.

## Thought 39—How Can I Give You Up?

*How can I give you up, Ephraim? How can I hand you over, Israel? How can I make you like Admah? How can I set you like Zeboiim? My heart churns within Me; My sympathy is stirred.*

Hosea 11:8

Have you ever asked the question, *Have I sinned away my salvation? My sins are so repetitive, how could God still love me?*

If that's you, you need to read the Book of Hosea. The prophet is commanded by God to marry a prostitute called Gomer—not a reformed prostitute; in fact, Gomer would still repeatedly cheat on him, God said. Hosea was commanded to marry her anyway, as a picture of God's love for Israel. Though they were unfaithful to Him, He would remain faithful and never leave them nor forsake them.

The picture of marriage in Hosea is also a picture of parenthood. If you are a parent, go back to the days when you nursed a baby in your arms. You fed them, you clothed them, you held their hand as they learned to walk; they meant everything to you because they were your baby. However, that baby grew into a teenager who rebelled horribly against you. They spat abuse at you, stole from you, took drugs, and slept around. It got so bad that you said, "I can't go through this any longer; you have to leave; you can't live with us here anymore." So your child packs a big bag of clothes, walks down the stairs, and just as they open the door to leave, they look back at you and the heart of God which dwells within us all, your God-given conscience cries out, *How can I give you up?*

That's what God thinks every time you cheat on Him. *Yes, you've failed me; yes, you've played the prostitute again; but I cannot give you up. I love you too much. I can't rain fire and brimstone on you like those towns in Sodom and Gomorrah; Admah and Zeboiim* (see verse above). No, you're a daughter of Christ; you're a son of the Most High God. You were bought with a price and God will not give you up.

# Thought 40—Draw Near to Him

*Draw near to God and He will draw near to you.*

James 4:8

A couple of weeks ago, my eighteen-month-old son made me the happiest man in the world. He said, "Daddy, cuddle," and climbed across the bed to a semi-conscious me and gave me a big hug. There is no way I would ever say to my boy, "Go away," or "Not now, I'm busy." No, it filled my heart with happiness that my child wanted to draw near to me.

You are God's child, and He wants you to draw near to Him like a little child. I wonder, what is your prayer life like? Do you give God the very best hours of the day, the very crème de la crème, or do you give Him the cigarette butts of the day?

I cannot emphasize this enough—you will never overcome this besetting sin without daily wrestling with God in prayer. If we are prayerless, we are graceless. But never get the idea that prayer is a burden. To experience a Father-and-child relationship with God every day, to pour your heart out to Him, and then to know the God of the universe is listening, is the most amazing feeling in the world!

But it starts with you taking a step toward God and He will take a step toward you. If I didn't speak to my wife for a week what would my marriage look like? *Terrible!* Yet sometimes we think we can ignore God for weeks and expect a spiritual breakthrough. The School of Life teaches us to draw near first, and then we will see a breakthrough.

## *Thought 41—God's Unconditional Love*

*For I am persuaded that neither death nor life, nor angels nor principalities nor powers, nor things present nor things to come, nor height nor depth, nor any other created thing, shall be able to separate us from the love of God which is in Christ Jesus our Lord.*

Romans 8:38–39

Imagine I'm standing in front of you and I pull out a crisp, clean $10 bill. The value of that bill is ten American dollars. Imagine then if I scrunched the money up into a ball, stepped on it, and covered it in manure. At the beginning the bill was worth $10. Now it's creased, now it's dirty—but what is the value of the bill? It's still $10. My dear friend, you may feel creased, dirty, stepped on. But you have still not lost your value in God's eyes. Why? Because you're washed in the blood of the Lord Jesus Christ. God is not like us. His love is not dependent on circumstances or feelings. No, His love is unconditional and He has loved you with an everlasting love. Today's Bible verse says that no "created thing shall be able to separate us from the love of God." Are you created? Yes, you are! So not even you can separate yourself from the love of God. Even if we are faithless, He will remain faithful. This is God demonstrating His deep love and grace. For it is by grace we have been saved.

# Thought 42—Are You a Pig?

*But it has happened to them according to the true proverb:
"A dog returns to his own vomit," and, "a sow, having
washed, to her wallowing in the mire."*

Second Peter 2:22

Never forget, we are to be ruthless with sin. I hope this question doesn't offend you, but are you a sheep? Or are you a pig? Supposing there's a large mud puddle. A sheep might get a little curious, draw close to the edge, and before it realizes it, it's fallen into the filth. As soon as it falls in, it climbs out of the mud and gets as far away from the puddle as possible. It's ashamed that its coat is dirty; it's a sheep. But when a pig sees a mud puddle, its eyes light up; it runs to the mud puddle and dives right in. In its free will, it remains there with no intention of getting out. it loves the filth; it's a pig. The sheep's nature is to be clean and pure. The pig's nature is to be dirty and to wallow in the mire.[15]

So let me ask you the question again: *Are you a sheep or a pig?* When you fall into sin, do you try to get back out? Do you try and get as far away from sin as possible when you sin? When you do fall, do you feel angry and ashamed? Do you sense that this is not your home, not your native habitat? Do you know this is not where you belong?

If the answer is yes, you're a sheep and you need to keep fighting this sin. The fact that you're nearly halfway through a book on purity is evidence there is a battle going on and you are not content to wallow in the mire. So keep fighting! Do not lose heart; remember, you're a sheep, but not a lone sheep. No, you have a Good Shepherd who will guide you away from all those mud puddles and will help to keep you clean until He takes you home to a place where there are no mud puddles to fall in.

# Thought 43—The Devil's Like the YouTube Algorithm

*Now the serpent was more cunning than any*
*beast of the field which the LORD God had made.*

Genesis 3:1

I'm often amazed at how YouTube knows more about what I'd like to watch than I do! Its algorithm is always presenting enticing videos related to my interests, to get me to click on them. For instance, I'm very interested in cold water swimming, so when I log onto YouTube, there on my home page are videos all about cold water swimming that are too intriguing for me to resist, even when I'm supposed to be working!

YouTube knows exactly what to present in front of us to get clicks—and so does the Devil. He knows what tempts you better than you know yourself. In the battle against lust there's always a trigger point, and the crafty serpent knows which of your multiple trigger points will work in each particular situation.

It is different for different people. In one man, flattery is enough to poison the mind to lead him into sin. In another, discouragement will drive him into a need to self-soothe with sin. Just like Jesus is a fisher for men, Christ's enemy Lucifer is also a fisher of men and he will dangle all kinds of bait in your face all day long to get you to click on wrong images, or think evil thoughts, or even put yourself in wrong situations. So today, write down your trigger points, because once you know your Achilles heel, you will know how to guard against it when the Evil One comes knocking at your door.

## *Thought 44—Guess Who My Favorite Bible Character Is*

*So the captain came to him, and said to him, "What
do you mean, sleeper? Arise, call on your God; perhaps
your God will consider us, so that we may not perish."*

Jonah 1:6

Sometimes when I preach at a church I ask the congregation, "Who do you think my favorite Bible character is, outside of Jesus Christ?" I hear them throw out names like Paul, Samson, Daniel, or David. But do you know who I like more than them? The sea captain in the story of Jonah. Here in the story we have Jonah asleep on the bottom deck of the ship, while the storm rages and the sailors on the top deck are fighting for their lives. The sea captain, who was not a believer, rebukes the believer Jonah and tells him to call on his God. So in other words, an unbeliever was telling the man of God what he should be doing. The reason it resonates so strongly with me is I remember times in my life where an unbelieving work colleague or family member has told me a story and I laughed inappropriately. Often they would say the same thing: "Why are you acting like that—you're supposed to be a Christian."

If you struggle with lust, you must also get rid of crude jokes and laughing at inappropriate things with your friends or coworkers, because a scary sign we've backslidden is when unbelievers start telling us what we should be doing. You see, the world, as blind and immoral as it is, still holds up a standard to the Christian and when we don't meet that standard they will soon let you know. So remember, wherever you go you are an ambassador for Christ.

## *Thought 45—Complete in Christ*

*Then the rib which the L&#1013;RD God had taken from man*
*He made into a woman, and He brought her to the man.*

Genesis 2:22

Y ou know the story well. When God created woman, He put Adam into a deep sleep, almost like a coma. He then removed a rib from Adam and created woman from that rib. As Matthew Henry famously said 'The woman was made of a rib out of the side of Adam; not made out of his head, to rule over him, nor out of his feet, to be trampled upon by him, but out of his side, to be equal with him, under his arm to be protected, and near his heart to be beloved.'[16] So from that day on, Adam was missing something—he was incomplete. And a lot of men (but not all!) also feel something is missing. That's why, ladies, your husband "isn't all there." But when a man gets married, his lost rib is re-joined. He was incomplete when he did not have a wife, but once he found her, he was made whole.

This is a picture of the cross. Jesus Christ, the second Adam, was crucified for our sins on the cross. When it was all over a Roman soldier wanted to check that Jesus was really dead and so he plunged a spear into Christ's side. Just like Eve came from Adam's side and he was later joined together in marriage to his bride, so we the church have come from Jesus' side. From the price that was paid at the cross we are now the Bride of Christ and we are made complete in Him. So whether you're married or not, you are made whole in Him and one day you will eat at the marriage supper of the Lamb. You may never have been invited to a wedding, but if you're married to Christ, you'll definitely be going to this one!

## Thought 46—Jesus Is the Glue

*"And the two shall become one flesh"; so then*
*they are no longer two, but one flesh.*

Mark 10:8

Suppose I took a piece of super-strong adhesive tape and stuck it on your arm. As long as no one tampers with it, it will stay there forever. But what happens if I rip it off and then stick it on your other arm? It will still be strong but it won't be as sticky as it was the first time. What if I repeat the process three, four, five, six, seven times? What's going to happen by the seventh time? Well, eventually, it won't be able to stick to anything. That's how God created you and me. We were designed to be bound, joined together with just one person for life. But the more people we have sex with, the harder it is to find a lasting bond. Our modern-day culture has cheapened sex and made it as trivial as brushing your teeth, but the Bible teaches that when a man and woman come together in intercourse that it's not just physical but two souls coming together. That's why the Scripture says, "Whoever commits adultery with a woman lacks understanding; He who does so destroys his own soul" (Prov. 6:32).

So if you're a virgin, I plead with you to guard this precious gift with your life. But what if you're not? Is there still hope for you? Yes, with Jesus there is always hope. Christ can come in and be the glue. He can take that lifeless, creased piece of tape and bind it to another flesh for life. His blood washes away the sins of our past and He then clothes your naked body, which is ashamed, in His righteous garment. And His cloak of righteous is one size that fits all. Although some of us made a real mess before marriage, God can make us pure again and join us with another in marriage. And never forget, "What therefore God has joined together let not man separate" (Mark 10:9).

## Thought 47—Sealed by the Holy Spirit

*And do not grieve the Holy Spirit of God,*
*by whom you were sealed for the day of redemption.*

Ephesians 4:30

The verse above teaches us two things: the Holy Spirit is strong and the Holy Spirit is sensitive. First, if we are sealed by the Holy Spirit, nothing can break that bond. Once the Holy Spirit has occupied the house, there is no room for another. Moreover, if He seals a vessel nothing can come in and nothing can get out. So, if you're born again, take comfort that you are glued to the Spirit of God until Jesus returns. God's glue is much stronger than the Gorilla Glue you can buy at the local hardware store.

Second, remember the Holy Spirit is sensitive. A missionary couple moved to Jerusalem with the burden to see Jews accept the Messiah, Jesus Christ. Not long after they had bought a house they discovered there was a white dove living in their rooftop. They saw it as a sign, as a seal on their ministry, since the Scriptures often picture the Holy Spirit as a dove. But they soon realized that every time they argued, every time they slammed a door, the dove would fly away. Rather concerned, one day the husband said to his wife, "Either we adjust to the dove or the dove needs to adjust to us." The wife turned round with tears in her eyes and said, "I know. I'm frightened that one day we'll scare him off and he'll never come back." From that day on, the couple never argued.[17]

We will never truly lose the Holy Spirit once we are sealed, but that doesn't mean we can't grieve the Holy Spirit. When we sin, we are hurting the feelings of the Holy Spirit. The Holy Spirit is very sensitive and when you gossip, when you lose your temper, when you look at things you shouldn't; the dove flies away. When we sin we don't lose our salvation but we lose the presence of God. So make sure you are sensitive to the Holy Spirit in your conduct today.

58

### *Thought 48—Ask Jesus to Answer the Door*

*If you do well, will you not be accepted? And if you do not do well, sin lies at the door. And its desire is for you, but you should rule over it.*

Genesis 4:7

A Sunday school teacher one day sat down with her only student, a five-year-old girl. The teacher asked the girl, "Where does Jesus live?" The little girl replied, "He lives in my heart." The teacher, wanting to test the little girl, asked, "What do you do when the Devil comes and knocks on the door of your heart?" The little girl paused for a moment and then smiled. "I ask Jesus to open the door."

God's children need to remember this: Satan is crouching at the door; he wants to rule over you, to make you sin. So next time he knocks, ask Jesus to open the door. Why do we need Jesus? Because the Devil is older than us, he's smarter than us, he knows what tempts us, and he knows how to exploit us when we're weak. Though we are weak, thanks be to God that we know a strong Savior and just saying the very name "Jesus Christ" makes the demons shudder and tremble. And honestly, that's what I sometimes do when I'm tempted. I verbally pray out loud "Jesus Christ, help me; I know there is power in the name of Jesus Christ." Do I look crazy? Yes! But does it work? Yes! Should you try it? Absolutely!

## Thought 49—Nip Adultery in the Bud

*But I say to you that whoever looks at a woman to lust for her has already committed adultery with her in his heart.*

Matthew 5:28

Everyone knows cheating is wrong. We have television shows dedicated to it and even the people of the world are horrified when a man or woman commits adultery. But Jesus proves that there is none righteous, not even one, and although many of us would never cheat on our spouse we all have committed adultery in our hearts. According to God, lustful looks are not harmless but very serious, because sin begins in the mind. If we nourish bad thoughts, it leads to the act. I'm sure if we displayed the thoughts you and I have had in the last week on a huge screen and put it in the center of town, we'd both be totally ashamed. What's scary, though, is that the advertisers and entertainers of the world know that sex sells, so they exploit it; when we walk down a street, it's easy to commit adultery a dozen times! Billboards are sensual, music videos are saturated with soft-core pornography, and now, because of social media, modesty has been thrown out the window. We must train ourselves to stop mindlessly lusting in this impure culture. Remind yourself that sexualizing others is wrong and people aren't chunks of meat for your own gratification—no, they are souls made in the image of God.

## Thought 50—Radical Repentance

*And if your eye causes you to sin, pluck it out and cast it
from you. It is better for you to enter into life with one
eye, rather than having two eyes, to be cast into hell fire.*

Matthew 18:9

Sadly, this verse has been so misinterpreted by some people in the past that they have literally torn out their eye, thinking this would solve their sexual sin. I heard of a man who took the previous verse ("If your hand or foot causes you to sin, cut it off and cast it from you") literally and put his arm on a railway track, so he would not do sinful things with his hands anymore. But clearly, removing an eye or hand will not deal with the root of the issue. I heard the story of a pastor who used to counsel a blind man and what was the blind man's besetting sin? Lust.

When Jesus used this graphic illustration, he was saying we need to have a radical type of repentance; we should be ruthless with sin, not our bodies. Christ's body was mutilated on the cross, so we certainly don't need to mutilate our bodies, too.

So, what is radical repentance? It means finding and avoiding the enabler that allows you to sin. What activities, what routines, what devices, what places are leading you to sexual sin?

Perhaps I took this too far in my early twenties; when I first got married I had a difficult conversation with my bride and we decided not to have the Internet in the house. So for five years I had to go to local libraries or coffee shops if I needed to use a computer. And honestly, as inconvenient as this decision was, I'm glad we did it, because the Internet was the enabler for my sin. So take a moment now to consider what the enabler is for your sin. Then ask yourself, *Am I willing to radically change my life to stay pure?* So, if your laptop causes you to sin pluck it out and cast it from you. (But please don't send me the bill if you regret the decision in a week.)

## Thought 51—Sex in the City

*Flee sexual immorality. Every sin that a man
does is outside the body, but he who commits
sexual immorality sins against his own body.*

First Corinthians 6:18

I used to think that people in Bible times had it easier than we do. After all, they weren't bombarded with every lewd image that the Internet pushes in our face; they didn't have smart phones and televisions, all promoting sensuality. But I was wrong.

They didn't have the media we have, but the people of Corinth were one of the most sexualized cultures in history. Greco-Roman culture worshipped Aphrodite, the goddess of "love" (i.e., sex). Sexual liberty was rife, even compared to our modern-day culture. The apostle Paul was concerned about the church and some of the perverse sins being committed in it (see 1 Cor. 5), so he warned those living in the sexual city of Corinth to "flee sexual immorality" (6:18).

Just as Joseph had to physically escape Potiphar's wife when she begged him to sleep with her, so we, like Joseph, have to run from temptation. You may need to get out of the house to remove yourself from a situation. Joseph didn't even have time to get his coat back; he knew that staying in the place for even a fraction of a second would lead to a different ending. We, too, must have that same urgency to get away. Run, because the moment you linger you begin to rationalize the sin, and once that happens, you're dead in the water.

When a man steals, he sins with his hands; when a man gossips, he sins with his lips; but when a man commits sexual immorality, he sins with his whole body. The mind is engaged, the eyes gaze, the hands touch, the feet walk to the sin location, the loins burn, and the heart lusts. The whole body is betrothed to the work of impurity and that's why the whole body must run when sexual sin beckons its finger to you today.

## Thought 52—Reality Check

*Whoever has been born of God does not sin, for His seed remains in him; and he cannot sin, because he has been born of God.*

First John 3:9

In the Bible there is a tension. God is abundant in grace to sinners and has a longsuffering nature toward us, even though we fail Him many times. But on the flip side, there is His call to holiness—every one of us has a responsibility to repent and turn from our sins.

Here, in one of the most terrifying verses in the Bible, John sternly warns that no one born of God makes a practice of sinning. The Bible does not teach that if we mess up or backslide we will be eternally separated from God. But I do believe it does teach that if you make a craft of sinning, if it's a lifestyle, if like the pig you settle yourself into the mud and are content to practice sin, you have not been born of God. To practice sin is to do it continually with no change in direction. Of course, every believer falls and if we say we have no sin, we are saying God is a liar! So I pray that the fear of the Lord would keep us from habitual sin.

Those who refuse to repent and have spent every day indulging the lusts of the flesh should not be surprised at where they wake up when their time on earth is up.

# Thought 53—Satan's Three Secret Weapons

*For all that is in the world—the lust of the flesh, the lust of the eyes, and the pride of life—is not of the Father but is of the world.*

First John 2:16

Satan, who runs the world's system, has three secret weapons: the lust of the flesh, the lust of the eyes, and the pride of life. Every time he attacks he uses one of these to tempt us to sin.

We see this so clearly when the serpent tempted Eve in the Garden of Eden. The fruit of the tree was "good for food," appealing to the flesh's desire for luxury; it was "pleasant to the eyes," appealing to the eyes' desire to fixate on beauty; and the fruit of the tree would "make one wise," appealing to the pride of man to be seen as knowledgeable (Gen. 3:6).

We see the exact same pattern when the Devil tempted Christ in the wilderness. Satan said, "Command that these stones become bread" (Matt. 4:3), appealing to the flesh. Jesus was hungry during His fast, but He had a greater mission than satisfying the flesh. Satan showed Jesus "all the kingdoms of the world and their glory" (4:8), appealing to the eyes and the desire we have to own beautiful things. Satan also tempted Jesus into a prideful demonstration of His power (see 4:6) and baited Him with, "If you are the Son of God" (4:3, 6), appealing to the prideful desire in human nature to protect one's reputation.

One good thing about Satan's strategy is it's predictable. So spend some time today thinking about how you might be tempted by one of these three strategies.

## Thought 54—Don't Be Deceived

*For this you know, that no fornicator, unclean person, nor covetous man, who is an idolater, has any inheritance in the kingdom of Christ and God. Let no one deceive you with empty words, for because of these things the wrath of God comes upon the sons of disobedience.*

Ephesians 5:5–6

I remember doing a set of classes on purity with some men who were a little younger than I. When we read this Scripture together, one young man who always spoke his mind blurted out, "I had no idea this verse existed."

It doesn't get much plainer than this. Those who haven't repented of sexual sin will not have an inheritance with Christ, but can only expect the wrath of God. The wrath of God is not heaven, so we can conclude that this verse means it isn't just a case of losing a reward in heaven; those who live a totally impure life will go to hell.

I remember reading this verse for the first time, and trying to find a different interpretation that would take the edge off what it says. I was guilty, and like the other young man, I couldn't believe my eyes. But the proceeding line erases any opportunity for misunderstanding, "Let no one deceive you with empty words." Beware of flatterers. Many today will tell you what you want to hear so that they might exploit you for personal gain. But there is a day when mercy is cut off. I plead with you not to keep kicking sand in the face of God. Everyone around you may use the blood of Christ as a license for sin, but you're different. Don't be deceived by others. Ongoing rebellion against the living God is very serious.

## Thought 55—Keep Walking

*Yea, though I walk through the valley of the
shadow of death, I will fear no evil; For You are
with me; Your rod and Your staff, they comfort me.*

Psalm 23:4

David writes, "Yea, though I walk through the valley of the shadow of death." You may be wrestling with a serious illness, but you still have to keep walking; your home life might be falling apart, but you still have to keep walking; every day you may encounter the most vile temptations, but you still have to keep walking.

Why? Because lying defeated won't get you anywhere.

The great temptation is to feel sorry for ourselves after we've fallen into sin, but remember, self-pity will not help us get through the valley. The only option we have is to keep walking.

You may say, "I can't Joe; you have no idea how much I'm struggling right now." Just take one step at a time.

"One step!?" you may cry. "What good will one step do? The valley is deep, and the road is long!"

The Empire State Building was built one step at a time. The Notre Dame Cathedral was built one step at a time. Fix your eyes on the Lord Jesus and keep taking one step closer each day, and you will make it through this valley.

Notice it does not say, "I *run* through the valley of the shadow of death." The child of God is in no hurry. This trial, hard as it may be, has been permitted by the sovereign Lord for a reason. In our longing for purity, we want to rush through the pain and daily battles. But we must not rush the lectures of God, because when we finish we will gain a PhD in suffering, worth more than any degree from Harvard or Oxford, because it comes from the very hand of God. So when the pain and the battles come today, and they will come, remember to keep walking.

## *Thought 56—Accountability Is a Gift*

*Confess your trespasses to one another, and pray for
one another, that you may be healed. The effective,
fervent prayer of a righteous man avails much.*

James 5:16

I'm a big believer in accountability software. Sin thrives in secrecy. Once you confess your sin to a trusted brother or sister in Christ, you find a huge weight is lifted off your shoulders because your friend will help carry this burden with you. Accountability software works by blocking adult content and also by taking multiple screenshots every minute you are active on your device. It also records all your searches across the Internet, so that anything concerning or suspicious is forwarded to your accountability partner's email address.

As powerful as these tools are, though, they can only help so much. You're camping and you keep filling your water bottle from a river, but you notice the water is contaminated with blood. What's the most sensible thing to do? To filter every bucket out until the water is pure, or to walk upstream and remove the dead carcass contaminating the water? Once you deal with the heart of the problem, the water can flow clean again. Whatever the idol is that's contaminating your heart today, rip it from the throne of God and treasure Christ with every fiber of your being.

# Thought 57—Walking in the Spirit

*If we live in the Spirit, let us also walk in the Spirit.*

Galatians 5:25

One day a mother bought a pristine white dress for her little girl. The girl instantly wanted to show it off to all of her friends. Her mother agreed, under one condition. "You must not get the dress dirty." The little girl nodded her head and bounded outside with her friends. A few hours later, the little girl knocked on her mother's door, looking like a mud pie. The mother washed the dress and the next day she sent the little girl out to play with the same instructions. The little girl returned, even muddier.

This pattern repeated itself over and over again, until—what do you suppose happened? That little girl became a woman; she grew up to be like her mother. Over time the mother's spirit was imparted into the little girl, and she learned her mother's ways.

This is exactly what happens to us when we are born from above. The Holy Spirit teaches us to walk, but many times we get dirty. Eventually, though, if we keep seeking to walk by the Spirit, we'll walk around the mud instead of falling into it. The more we listen to the Holy Spirit's voice and obey His convictions in our conscience, the more He imparts His holiness into our lives.

## Thought 58 - Sin's Price Tag

*Immediately he went after her, as an ox goes to the*
*slaughter, Or as a fool to the correction of the stocks,*
*Till an arrow struck his liver. As a bird hastens to*
*the snare, He did not know it would cost his life.*

Proverbs 7:22–23

When I used to work in a café, on the till there was a button entitled "impulse buy." It was cleverly named, because all the stock that fitted into that category was conveniently stacked right next to the cash register. After the customer had ordered what they wanted off the menu, their eyes saw a tempting rocky road brownie or a bag of chips, and they bought them without any thought, as they only had seconds to make the decision. Many people impulse-buy from the Devil, not realizing the cost on the price tag. They make a rash decision in the moment, without realizing the consequences. The Bible says that just like an ox unconsciously walks itself to its death, and like a bird hops into its doom, so the deluded person who rushes to sin will have a miserable fate.

Does this mean if I keep committing sexual sin, I'm going to hell? Well, I believe there is always abundant grace in Jesus to be found for any repentant sinner. But I also believe that the Bible warns there is a dreadful price to pay for those who die refusing to let go of their chosen sin. Charles Bridges, commenting on this passage, referred to it as "the short night of pleasure succeeded by the eternal night of infernal torment!"[18]

I guess what I'm trying to say is, how much longer will you continue to play this game? Your soul is not a game, eternity is not a game, and God is certainly not an opponent any of us should challenge. So be cleansed today by the blood of Jesus, and be sure tomorrow you don't walk too close to the edge.

## *Thought 59—Put Your Sins in a Mortuary*

*Therefore put to death your members which are
on the earth: fornication, uncleanness, passion,
evil desire, and covetousness, which is idolatry.*

Colossians 3:5

Come with me and sit at the bedside of a dying man. Tell him who won last night's ball game. Tell him about the latest political crisis. Tell him that your favorite celebrity couple just got divorced. Tell him any new piece of worldly news or gossip, and see how much interest he shows. He doesn't care—he's a dying man on the brink of eternity, where his next life, in either heaven or hell, is about to begin.

In comparison, Paul commands the church of Colossae to put to death evil desire within the flesh. The Christian has a new life; the way of the old life should not fascinate us anymore, because we are dead to this world. Remember the old war movie scene where the commanding officer says, "Take no prisoners"? Paul, as a commanding officer, says the same thing to the flock of Christ. Don't think you can successfully harbor a dangerous enemy under your roof. He will one day stab you in the back when you least expect it. Sin is not our friend, and just like killing anything is not pleasant (in fact, it's extremely hard), we must show no mercy and put to death those wicked sins of the flesh.

## Thought 60—The War for Your Soul

*Beloved, I beg you as sojourners and pilgrims,*
*abstain from fleshly lusts which war against the soul.*

First Peter 2:11

A Christian friend once said this to me rather sternly: "Joe Kirby isn't who you see in the mirror; no, the real Joe Kirby is in your soul."

Your soul is the real you; it's your emotions, your personality, your will, your mind. It's no wonder the famous evangelist D.L. Moody said wryly, "I have had more trouble with D.L. Moody than with any other man who has crossed my path."[19]

Once we realize this, life starts to look a little less trivial. With every decision we make, we should ponder the question, *Is this good for my soul?* Does this career, friend, movie, social media platform, self-help guru, swimming outfit injure my soul? Choices that seem wise in the world's eyes are very often anti-God.

One of the worldly deceptions that kept me in the land of pornography for so long was the belief that "I need this." I would think, *I'm stressed out; I can't keep this level of stress in my body; I need something to relax me, to take the edge off life.* But it never did; in fact, it made me all the more stressed and anxious.

We can't commit an act of uncleanness and expect to come out totally unscathed. This verse is clear that fleshly lust will always leave a wound, a scar, a defilement on the soul, and the more we return to the uncleanness the more wounds our souls suffer. But the glorious truth of the Bible is that "by His stripes we are healed" (Isa. 53:5), and if we abstain from fleshly lusts, Jesus can sew that lacerated soul together and make it whole again in Christ.

## Thought 61—How Can a Young Man Stay Pure?

*How can a young man cleanse his way?*
*By taking heed according to Your word.*

Psalm 119:9

To quote D.L. Moody again, "This book [the Bible] will keep you from sin, or sin will keep you from this book.'[20] The simplest answer to how to overcome sexual sin is not accountability software, nor biblical counselling, nor even soliciting the prayers of godly people—though these are all wonderful and super-important in this battle. But the greatest thing a young man or woman can do to fight this sin is to get disciplined and spend quality time in the Word of God every day.

Discipline is hard, but if something is valuable to you, you'll find the discipline to make it happen. What would you do if I gave you $1,000 every week to memorize one of these verses on purity? I guarantee that in a year, you would be $52k richer! You may say, "Not me, Joe! My memory is like a sieve." Well, the Bible is described as water because it cleanses, so even if the verses don't stick, you will have a clean sieve by the end of the year! You may think I'm joking, but the Holy Spirit will bring these verses to mind at just the right time, and just the very action of reading the Word of God purifies our hearts and minds.

## *Thought 62—Big Macs and Sex*

*Foods for the stomach and the stomach for foods, but God
will destroy both it and them. Now the body is not for sexual
immorality but for the Lord, and the Lord for the body.*

First Corinthians 6:13

It is believed that in this verse Paul is dealing with an unhealthy mindset that the people of Corinth had adopted. They reasoned this way: *If your stomach desires food, eat as many different foods as you like; if your body desires sex, have sex with as many different people as you like* (an attitude not unheard-of even today). But Paul emphatically says, "No! The Christian's body is dedicated to the Lord."

I can eat a Big Mac, and though I may feel a little guilty about the calories, I can go about my daily life unharmed. However, when a person has intercourse, his mind, heart, and spirit become entwined. Every time those who fornicate give their body to another, it is like they are peeling an onion; they lose a layer of themselves, and tears often follow. Repeat this process often enough and what happens to the onion? It's empty, with nothing left to give. That's why if you ask a seasoned fornicator if it was worth it, they will often respond, "I don't know who I am anymore, I feel lost." Well, praise God, we worship a Savior who came to seek and save the lost, and all those who trust in Him and submit their lives to Him can be sure their lives are safe in His hands. And if you let Him, those hands will slowly rebuild the layers that were lost to the wastefulness of sin.

## Thought 63—Stop Robbing Your Own Bank!

*Stolen water is sweet, And bread eaten in secret is pleasant.*

Proverbs 9:17

Statistics have proven that crime really doesn't pay: the average amount stolen by bank robbers in the UK is £12,900.[21] To put this in perspective, at the date I'm writing this, the average salary in the UK is more than double that: £26,000. Bank robbers nearly always get caught, and serve an average of twelve years in prison. Twelve years? For less than half the average wage? Doesn't seem like a fair trade-off, does it? "Stolen water is sweet"—meaning it tastes good to eat what you shouldn't—but remember the prison sentence that almost always follows!

Those who who commit sexual sin are like bank robbers— they often end up in a prison of their own mind, thoughts, and self-loathing. And yet, sex inside of marriage is like *putting money in the bank*—it only grows over time. The connection runs deeper, the sex is more enjoyable, and God fills the couple with more of His love. So don't be tempted to have a quick heist here, or steal a little lust from the Internet there. It may feel exciting to begin with, but once you're in that jail cell, all you will feel is regret. Rather, we should cling to the Savior who sets the captives free!

## Thought 64—Would You Die for Jesus?

*I affirm, by the boasting in you which I*
*have in Christ Jesus our Lord, I die daily.*

First Corinthians 15:31

In *Foxe's Book of Martyrs* we read of Christians who sang hymns to Christ while being burned alive. The apostle Paul said, "We are killed all day long" (Rom. 8:36). And around the world today, more are dying for thier faith in Christ than ever before.

Many Christians read stories like that and say, "Wouldn't it be amazing to take a hit for Jesus? What an honor to be martyred for my Savior." Christianity may seem dull and lifeless and we seem to sacrifice so little here in the West.

If you're nodding your head and saying "Amen" right now, did you know there is a way for you personally to also have the honor of sacrifice and self-denial for the Lord? It's called obedience.

We say we'd die for Jesus tomorrow, but we aren't willing to live for Him today. If you want to be crucified for Christ, first crucify your passions on the cross for Jesus. If you want to take a radical stand for your God, first stand up to your flesh and say, "No more will I bow the knee to my selfish desires." A day may come, sooner than we think, when we will suffer real persecution and perhaps physically die for Jesus, but I believe the ones who will endure that day are the ones who are already dying to self and choosing Christ over their cravings.

## Thought 65—Jesus Shouldn't Be There

*I have been crucified with Christ; it is no longer I who live, but*
*Christ lives in me; and the life which I now live in the flesh I live*
*by faith in the Son of God, who loved me and gave himself for me.*

Galatians 2:20

Quite possibly the most incredible doctrine in the Bible is union with Christ. The infinite God of the universe chooses to live inside weak, fragile, earthen vessels like us!

How does this apply to purity? In our motivation. Many of our motivations to stop us from sinning are man-centered. We know that the way of the sinner is hard, and we do not want the ramifications that come to those who rebel against God. However, our greatest motivation should not be about us, but about God.

To put it bluntly, if Christ lives in you, then when you watch filth on the Internet, or fornicate, or listen to crude music, you take Jesus with you. The holy Son of God who has never sinned is brought into the center of wickedness every time you choose sin over holiness. It's no wonder you feel like you've been torn in two after yielding to sexual sin—the source of purity is being carried into total impurity. I find this hard to write, and I'm sure you find it hard to read—but let this shake us up.

The next time you want to watch pornography, remember that Jesus will be watching it with you. Picture Him standing next to you, crying, "I died for you, to set you free from the snares of sin; turn it off for Me." The next time you're tempted to sleep with a girlfriend or boyfriend, picture Christ in the room, hurting as He sees your disobedience. May God have mercy on us, that we would not be so self-centered, because Jesus Christ deserves better than the places we take Him when we sin.

## Thought 66—Every Day Is a New Page

*Through the LORD's mercies we are not consumed,*
*Because His compassions fail not. They are new*
*every morning; Great is Your faithfulness.*

Lamentations 3:22–23

When I first got saved, I remember approaching the former pastor of my church and saying, "Pastor David, I'm really struggling with lust. I keep going back to the same sin and just when I think I've beaten it, I fall again."

He looked at me with kind eyes and said, "Joe, did you read the Ladybird books when you were a child? You know, the books with a little red ladybird on the spine?"

"Yes, I did, Pastor," I replied.

"Well, those books had a very special motto, and it went like this: 'Every day is a new page.' Joe, that's how the Christian should live his life. 'Yesterday, Lord, I failed You. But today is a new page.'"

You know, I can't put it better than my old pastor friend. Every day is a new page, regardless of what you did yesterday, because God's mercy is bigger. No one's sin has ever made God unfaithful. Great is His faithfulness! The prophet Jeremiah encourages us that the Lord's mercies are new every morning. So today you have a fresh chance to be renewed, a fresh chance to repent, a fresh chance to serve God. We must never forget that we don't have the right to another hour. If only we knew the value of every single day, like someone with terminal cancer, we would live differently, we would pray differently, we would be grateful that today we are part of the land of the living and today we can rejoice in the abundant mercy of God.

## Thought 67—A Strong Warning

*Her feet go down to death, Her steps lay hold of hell.*

Proverbs 5:5

In J.R.R. Tolkien's novel *The Two Towers*, we read about a deceitful character called Gollum tricking two young hobbits, Frodo and Samwise Gamgee, by taking them up the treacherous steps to the lair of Shelob, the hungry female spider.[22] In the Bible verse for today, King Solomon also paints a terrifying picture that if we keep walking the steps of sexual immorality, those steps will ultimately lead to hell. It's a serious business to sin against a holy God, and Revelation 21:8 warns us that the sexually immoral will be consigned to the fiery lake of burning sulphur.

What would you think of a man who bought a plane ticket, but did not know where the plane's final destination was? Yet many a man or woman buys a plane ticket from the Devil, not realizing he is flying the plane straight into the bowels of hell. As Christians we are to take the hand of Christ so He can lead us to His still waters, but sometimes instead we let go and fall into ditches.

I suppose the question I'm asking you is, who's leading you the majority of your life—is it the immoral man or woman? Or is it the Lord Jesus Christ? If you know you're being led into the spider's lair, take heed from the book of Revelation again: "Remember therefore from where you have fallen; repent and do the first works, or else I will come to you quickly and remove your lampstand from its place—unless you repent" (Rev. 2:5).

## Thought 68—Daytime Revellers

*But these, like natural brute beasts made to be caught and destroyed ... and will receive the wages of unrighteousness, as those who count it pleasure to carouse in the daytime. They are spots and blemishes, carousing in their own deceptions while they feast with you*

Second Peter 2:12–13

At the date I write this one of the most disturbing crimes I have ever heard about has just happened. When you read the depths of the culprit's depravity, it reminds me of Peter's description of the false teachers of the day: "like natural brute beasts." If our children grow up hearing every day at school "You're an animal, you're an animal, we descended from animals," is it any wonder that when they grow up they live like animals? These false teachers were not only indulging in their pleasures in the cover of darkness but they were sinning in broad daylight. While other honest men were soberly working on their occupations these men were bathing in lust. These same wicked men probably pleaded for funds for their ministry from the hardworking Christians who worked during the day.

What do your days look like? Do you live soberly? If not, aren't you ashamed to revel in the daylight? When a believer becomes a creature of lust they stop living in the Spirit and they live in the flesh. Their eyes are set on flesh and they become like irrational animals making foolish decisions. But the Christian has a higher calling. We know we are not animals, we have been clothed in the righteousness of Christ, and we are indwelled by the Holy Spirit. So let us live up to this high calling and not be daytime revelers but rather children of the light.

### *Thought 69—Has God Wooed You?*

*Therefore, behold, I will allure her,*
*Will bring her into the wilderness,*
*And speak comfort to her.*

Hosea 2:14

Warren Wiersbe in his Study Bible writes, "God doesn't try to force His people to love Him. Instead, He woos."[23] Wooing is an old-fashioned term for courtship before marriage, meaning a man seeks to win the affections of a woman and show her that he loves her. God is still wooing people today, seeking that they be married to Him.

Very often we have a negative view of God, that He is some big cruel ogre waiting to dish out judgment, but the God of the Bible is incredibly patient. We later read in Hosea that God "drew them with gentle cords, with bands of love" (Hos. 11:4). May we all feel those gentle cords of love today.

The God of the universe longs for a relationship with you; when we run from Him, His heart aches. Satan would have you in chains to keep you under his rule, but God wants to set you free. If today you feel the love of God whispering in your ear, "Turn back to me," do not resist His call. Do not believe the lie from hell that God hates you, for He has loved you with an everlasting love. We often forget that God wants us in heaven more than we want to be in heaven, and if you don't believe me just look at the cross. God says you are His bride, so run back to the patient Bridegroom who will never stop loving you.

## Thought 70—Don't Blame God

*Let no one say when he is tempted, "I am tempted by God";*
*for God cannot be tempted by evil, nor does He Himself*
*tempt anyone. But each one is tempted when he is*
*drawn away by his own desires and enticed.*

James 1:13–14

I'm sure we've all heard someone play the blame game: "It's not my fault! So-and-so made me do it." Perhaps you find yourself blaming your friends or siblings when you get into trouble. But have you ever blamed God for your sin? In the few years I've been in ministry I've heard many kinds of people play the blame game. Some say, "Why did God give me these desires?" Some say, "Why doesn't God just remove this sin from my life? I've called out to Him, but He is ignoring me." I heard one man's wife on the radio say that when she caught her husband watching pornography his response was, "I can't help it; women are just too gorgeous."

Some don't blame God or women, but the Devil and his workers. "Satan made me do it," was Eve's first excuse for her sin; sadly, this excuse is becoming more and more popular among young Christians. People often email me about their lust struggles and it is not uncommon for them to ask me for deliverance. They believe there is a demon of lust making them sin, and if the demon is cast out they will stop sinning. In my experience, if a person returns to the sin these "deliverance minsters" claim it's because the demon has come back.

But James dismisses all of these excuses! "But each one is tempted when he is drawn away by his own desires and enticed" (1:14). You choose to sin when you listen to your own sinful flesh's desires. God tests us, but He never tempts us. And although Satan is the Tempter, he cannot force you to sin. The responsibility is with you, believer, and if we are honest, we know Satan doesn't need to tempt us; we go looking for trouble on our own.

## *Thought 71 –Abundantly Adulterous Eyes*

*Having eyes full of adultery and that cannot cease from*
*sin, enticing unstable souls. They have a heart trained*
*in covetous practices, and are accursed children.*

Second Peter 2:14

I wonder—what goes through your mind when someone attractive walks past you? Where do your eyes move to? Are you disciplined in that moment, or do you lack self-control?

In Second Peter, the apostle describes false teachers who, like Olympic athletes, have trained themselves to scan every woman who walks by and engage in lustful fantasy. Their eyes are "*full* of adultery" (the literal meaning is "beyond quantity"); in other words, all these men see is sex. It's what they think about while eating and working; it's their first thought in the morning and their last at night. They are greedy individuals in general, but their greatest greed isn't for money or possessions, but for someone else's wife.

The reality is, every day something tempting catches our eyes, whether it's on our smart phone, in the street or even at church! But do you look away? These false teachers didn't. They may have claimed they were unable to stop, but they festered on what they saw and invited it into their imagination. However, the true believer should learn to obey the voice of the Holy Spirit. If the eyes and heart can be trained to be instruments of lust, can we not reverse that and train them to be instruments of righteousness?

## *Thought 72—Spiritual Toothpaste*

*Blessed is the man who endures temptation; for when*
*he has been approved, he will receive the crown of life*
*which the Lord has promised to those who love Him.*

James 1:12

Christians are like tubes of spiritual toothpaste—pressure brings out what's really on the inside! Or if you prefer this illustration, we are all like tea bags—when we're dropped in hot water it brings out our true colors. We've all dropped a stale tea bag in hot water, only to see there wasn't much goodness left; it brewed, but nothing really came out. So when we are under strain due to pressure or trials, let's not be seen as counterfeit Christians. The believer who endures patiently and depends upon the Lord through the difficulty is promised to receive the crown of life. What a motivation that should be to drive us to discipline ourselves, to be crowned by the Lord Himself in glory!

Nothing worthwhile was ever achieved without discipline, nor was any worthwhile achievement maintained without discipline. Many people have ruined their lives by growing slack. Imagine if William Wilberforce had given up when he sought to abolish slavery in 1807. Despite great resistance, by continual perseverance over twenty-six years, Wilberforce eventually saw slavery abolished in 1833. Spurgeon said, "By perseverance the snail reached the ark."[24]

I don't know what trial you're going through right now, but I do know in my own life how many times I turned to sin for comfort, and it only made matters worse. Let Christ be your rod and staff as you suffer, for the storms of life only make the tree grow stronger.

## Thought 73—Two Classes of People

*For those who live according to the flesh set their minds on the things of the flesh, but those who live according to the Spirit, the things of the Spirit.*

Romans 8:5

After the Titanic sank in 1912, the White Star Line put a big sign outside its ferry office listing two classes of people: "Known to be saved" and "Known to be lost."

That couldn't be more true. There are only two camps of people in this world—those who are "known to be saved," who live according to the Spirit, and those who are "known to be lost," who set their minds on the things of the flesh. All through the Bible this picture continues in different forms: sheep and goats, wheat and tares, good trees and bad trees, the narrow way and the broad way, and those written in the Lamb's book of life and those who are not.

Which class are you in? This verse is clear: Those who live according to the Spirit have been radically changed; they are not perfect, but those justified by faith in Christ do not live as they once did. As Christians we can't live with one foot in the world and one foot in the Kingdom. We can't sit on the fence, nor can we live like a believer Monday to Friday and unregenerate on the weekend. Why? Because we are no longer taken up with the things of this world. The carnal live like a tree that has for many years been bent by by the wind: their appetites have focused them in one direction. But we are like the tree in Psalm 1 with roots nourished by the rivers of grace, and we spread upwards with our eyes on our Maker above.

## Thought 74—Losing the Joy

*Restore to me the joy of Your salvation,*
*And uphold me by Your generous Spirit.*

Psalm 51:12

When we sin, we do not lose our salvation, we lose the *joy* of our salvation. (The verse actually says "*Your* salvation"—salvation belongs to the Lord. If it were in our hands, we could lose it, but since it's in God's hands, it is eternally secure.)

Remember how joyful you were when you first came to Christ? The celebration that a soul has been reconnected with its Maker produces an unfathomable joy! I know a man who was thought to have "lost his marbles" when he first became a Christian, because he couldn't stop smiling. We sometimes overlook what the angel proclaimed to the shepherds: "Behold, I bring you good tidings of great joy, which shall be to all people" (Luke 2:10). To be saved by Christ Jesus is the happiest fact the human heart can know.

But sadly, we like David probably know what it is to have that joy fade, to watch it disintegrate into thin air. When we live in sin and lack repentance, we break fellowship with God and we lose the blessed joy we once knew. How do we get it back? We confess our sin, like David did; we truly turn from it and ask God to restore the joy of His salvation. No one but God can give you back this joy, so wait upon the Lord until He hears your cries.

## Thought 75—The Sixth Commandment

*You shall not commit adultery.*

Exodus 20:14

If by any chance there is someone reading this who is contemplating an affair, I want to urge you right now, *don't do it!*

You will end up wishing you had enough money to buy every clock in the world, in the hope that one of them had the power to turn back time. But it's too late—adultery is irreversible, and leaves scars that run deep, generation after generation.

God takes adultery seriously—the Old Testament punishment was death by stoning. Yet today we are "entertained" by adultery. It seems like nearly every Hollywood film has a secret affair in the sub-plot. Reality-TV shows like *Cheaters* feed off the details of affairs. Even at work it seems everyone in the company knows about Johnny's infidelity—except maybe his wife.

We should be embarrassed to hear about cheating spouses when the Devil dangles such gossip in our ears. "'For it is shameful even to speak of those things which are done by them in secret" (Eph. 5:12). And let no one think they are immune to affairs, no matter how old they may be. Stay close to your spouse; remember the vows you made before the eyes of the Lord. It is said a successful marriage is about falling in love many times—but it's always with the same person!

## Thought 76—God's Escape Routes

*God is faithful, who will not allow you to be tempted*
*beyond what you are able, but with the temptation will*
*also make the way of escape, that you may be able to bear it.*

First Corinthians 10:13

The Hillsborough Disaster is a well-known tragedy in English sport. One of the tunnel gates was opened to ease overcrowding, which only forced a huge influx of people into the stadium. Sadly, 97 soccer fans were crushed to death in the Hillsborough stadium, and 766 people injured.

I had the privilege of meeting a Hillsborough survivor. He said that thirty years later he still suffers nightmares, and whenever he enters a room the first thing he looks for is the exit.

As Christians, whenever we walk into a temptation we, too, should look for the exit, because God always prepares a way out. To my shame, I have often ignored these ladders of escape. These exit points vary, but sometimes a Christian song comes to mind in the middle of the act, or perhaps someone knocks on the door, or some other interruption occurs. Of course, immediately after you've indulged in the sin, it's easy to recognize where God's exit point was at the beginning of the temptation. We often ask God to remove the temptation from us, but when He provides the escape route, do we take it? If you see no obvious way out, call on the name of Jesus Christ. He was tempted in every way and was triumphant over all sin. Just as a sheep is never attacked while it stands at the shepherd's side, no saint has ever been hardened by Satan's schemes while standing next to the Good Shepherd's side. Christ is the Doctor, but He's also the medicine!

# Thought 77—Let Me Take a Selfie!

*So Samuel said, "When you were little in your*
*own eyes, were you not head of the tribes of Israel?*
*And did not the LORD anoint you king over Israel?*

First Samuel 15:17

You probably know the story well. Saul was anointed as the first king over Israel; as long as he was meek, and saw himself unworthy to be a servant of God, he saw the Lord's blessing on his life. But over time, Saul's heart became corrupted by self-importance and it turned him to sin and arrogance. We should daily be seeking to only view ourselves as small in our own eyes, because far too often many people see themselves as large in their own eyes.

When my parents were young, they used to go to a national park to view a waterfall; they took a picture of it, and were staggered by the beauty of the waterfall every time they looked at the photo. Today, while visiting this park, many people take a "selfie" with the waterfall behind them. Suddenly, the focus of the photo isn't the large, beautiful waterfall, but their large head and this tiny waterfall in the background.

Where is your focus? On yourself or the magnitude of Christ? When we see ourselves as big in our eyes, we are easily deceived into believing we deserve this release, we deserve that pleasure, because we've worked hard and we need to unwind. But what we call "self-care" is really just selfishness. Let's take our eyes off self and fix our eyes on the vastness of Christ, and our fleshly desires will seem insignificant compared to obeying this vast God.

## Thought 78—Carrying Corpses

*There is a way that seems right to a man,*
*But its end is the way of death.*

Proverbs 14:12

There is nothing worse than a man or woman who is "wise in their own eyes" (Isa. 5:21). We want to carve out our own paths, and for many that means sowing some wild oats on the way. Everyone thinks they have the best recipe for a life well lived, but the Bible shows us the plans of men always have a bitter end.

In Roman mythology King Mezentius was an evil king who enjoyed torturing his captives. Instead of executing his victims, he tied dead corpses to the living. Mezentius' subjects were condemned to carry the dead body with them wherever they went until eventually the rotting corpse spread its decay to them and killed them also. Many Christians have been set free from the decaying sins they once knew, yet they insist on still carrying them, even though they are now new creations. Jesus said, "If the Son makes you free, you shall be free indeed" (John 8:36). Our sin is a choice; we can tie ourselves to this dead man until it leads us back to death, or we can bury those sins and leave them in the ground. It might be tempting to occasionally pick that sin up and cuddle it for a while, but the Bible says it's death. If Christ has cut the cords of sin, do not return to it, lest the second binding be worse than the first.

## Thought 79—Exercise Is Biblical

*For bodily exercise profits a little, but godliness is
profitable for all things, having promise of the
life that now is and of that which is to come.*

First Timothy 4:8

As Christians, our primary concern is the spiritual health of the soul; however, Paul here states there is a small benefit to exercising. We aren't to be like the world, worshipping our bodies, but we also mustn't forget we are physical creatures.

All the experts tell us that the greatest way to beat an addiction is regular exercise. Why is that? Because if you are addicted to pornography, you are actually addicted to dopamine. Dopamine is the pleasure hormone. God created it, but like most things in life the Devil has corrupted it. A conversation, marital sex, chocolate, cold showers, listening to music, and yes, exercise, all release dopamine. If over many years you have made a habit of sexual sin, you need to replace that habit with a new one—one that will produce equal pleasure, but a pure type of pleasure. Why do many intelligent adults rise at 5 a.m. to go running on a rainy Monday morning? Because an hour afterward their body releases happy hormones, giving them a "runner's high." Exercise is good for the body because God did not design us to be sedentary, so think about how you can practically incorporate exercise into your daily routine. (Personally, what I've found helpful is cold water swimming (as low as 40°F). I get a real buzz from it, but we're not all that weird.)

## Thought 80—Bored Believers

*As a loving deer and a graceful doe, Let her breasts satisfy you at all times; And always be enraptured with her love.*

Proverbs 5:19

This is the one verse you don't want your pastor to ask you to read out loud in a Bible study; it makes us blush. But why does Solomon command this man to only be satisfied with his wife's body, to always be enraptured by her love alone? Because sadly, within most men there is a susceptibility to get bored easily. Why do rich men buy a new sports car every month? Why do many pro athletes go through women like hot dinners? Why are men obsessed by the latest gadget? The answer is, most men are easily discontented.

Just this week I heard an interview with a preacher who said that for years he couldn't find the right woman to marry; he would date one for a few months, then get bored. Satan has exploited this flaw in men by providing men (and discontented women) with a plethora of exciting, fresh bodies to fixate over on the Internet. Whatever your sexual preference, you can find it on the web. It's called a web because once you're on it you can't get off, until that big evil spider comes along and sucks the life out of you. If you're married, thank God every day for the beauty of your wife. If you're not married and burn with lust, actively seek a wife if you haven't begun to already. Here's the beautiful thing about marriage: the more intimacy you have with your spouse, the more the connection and the attraction grows. On the flip side however, the more you gaze at other people's bodies, the more dissatisfied you become—not only with your spouse, but with life in general. What used to excite you now bores you, until your appetites get weirder and weirder.

## Thought 81—Hungry for God?

*Blessed are those who hunger and thirst for*
*righteousness, For they shall be filled.*

Matthew 5:6

A thirsty man stands still at the edge of the seashore with an empty jar as the tide is coming in. The man remains stationary as the sea washes over him and eventually the ocean fills his vessel with seawater. The man is so thirsty he takes the jar and drinks from it. The salt water leaves a bitter taste in his mouth and does not satisfy. The next day the man is still thirsty, so he climbs to the top of a steep mountain in search of a beautiful waterfall. When he finds it, he takes his jar and fills it up in the pure, flowing water. Again the man drinks from the jar, but this time it tastes sweet and refreshing.

That man is you! If you stand still, you will soon stagnate in your Christianity. Every day your soul must be filled with something; if you are not actively filling it up with the living waters of Christ, there is a sea of addictions and temptations waiting to fill your vessel. It's easy to stand still and be entertained by the lusts of this life, but drinking from broken cisterns that cannot hold water always leaves a bitter taste. However, if we go to the hard effort of climbing the spiritual mountain, seeking Christ's face every day in prayer and study, He will reward us with His sweet graces, which will never leave us disappointed. Mining for gold is always tough, but once found, the benefits far outweigh the sacrifice. So today let's get in the *Word* —before the *world* gets into us!

## Thought 82—You're Still Alive!

*He who has the Son has life; he who does*
*not have the Son of God does not have life.*

First John 5:12

Many Christians look at their performance, see their imperfect repentance, and begin to doubt if they ever began the race in the first place. But if a nurse takes the pulse of a weak man and his heart is beating faintly, is that man still alive? Of course he is! Likewise, your heart might be faintly beating for the things of God, but you must not assume you are still dead in your trespasses and sins. Instead, you need to exercise yourself unto godliness, to strengthen your spiritual heart through prayer, study, and fellowship.

Once God imputes life into the human soul, He does not retract it. How can we sit in the heavenly places on Tuesday, but make our bed in Sheol on Friday? How can our sins be removed and buried at the bottom of sea today, but tomorrow we stand condemned in the presence of God? We all go through seasons of doubt and unbelief because of our failings, but I want to remind you to keep your eyes on Christ and remember you are saved by grace alone! The next time the Devil whispers these thoughts in your ear, write this little acronym down: **G.R.A.C.E.—G**od's **R**iches **A**t **C**hrist's **E**xpense.

## Thought 83—Sweetness in Christ

*For the lips of an immoral woman drip honey,*
*And her mouth is smoother than oil;*
*But in the end she is bitter as wormwood,*
*Sharp as a two-edged sword.*

Proverbs 5:3–4

The Bible is the most honest book on earth. The Bible does not lie and try to cover the truth like other books do when they try to promote their own agenda. No, the Bible bluntly says sin is sweet, there is pleasure in sin, and lust does taste sweet in the beginning. The English clergyman William Gurnall said, "What lust is so sweet or profitable that is worth burning in hell for?"[25] The smoothness of sexual sin quickly turns abrasive, and if we go against the grain of God's laws we will get splinters.

However, there is a sweetness that never fades—the sweetness is found in Christ alone. He can transform the foulest situation into something beautiful. Consider Samson's lion carcass with me (see Judges 14). What could be more ugly than a dead, rotting lion, decomposing in the dry, arid wilderness? But what did Samson find in that carcass? A beehive that oozed delicious honey. This reminds us that with Christ there is always a sweetness in death. Although death is the final enemy, Christ has defeated that enemy when He triumphed over the grave. For the believer there is always sweetness when we finish, for Christ has removed the sting of death. Lust's sweetness quickly evaporates, but Christ's sweetness is unceasing, like the vastest ocean. Whose sweetness will you explore today?

## *Thought 84—Enemy of God*

*Adulterers and adulteresses! Do you not know that friendship with the world is enmity with God? Whoever therefore wants to be a friend of the world makes himself an enemy of God.*

James 4:4

Imagine a friend is having a conversation with you and the whole way through he has spoken to you in loving terms, but then suddenly, out of the blue, he calls you an adulterer, a cheater!

How would you react? You would be shocked to say the least, and yet that's exactly what James has done in his letter here. From referring to the readers gently with the words "my brethren" (James 3:1) all the way through, he suddenly changes the tone and calls the readers as unfaithful wives and husbands.

Spiritual adultery is a very serious crime in the eyes of the Lord. If you love the world and bathe in its pleasures, James states you are an enemy of God.

If an invisible video camera followed us every minute of every day for a week, what would that camera reveal? Would it show that our priorities lie with Christ's glory and His kingdom? Or would it capture us cuddling up to worldliness, perhaps even doing shameful things in secret?

In Ezekiel 14, we read of the elders of Israel committing spiritual adultery. To the onlookers they looked holy and spiritual, but to the Lord they were seen as hypocrites. So God told them to repent and turn from their idols. Is there an idol that has captured your heart recently? God is also calling you to repent today.

## *Thought 85—Playing with Fire*

*Can a man take fire to his bosom, And his clothes not be burned?*

Proverbs 6:27

When I was young believer, my two Indian friends and I would go for walks in a local park and confess our failings to one another in this area of pornography. I'll never forget when the oldest of my friends looked at me quite severely and said in his strong Indian accent, "If you play with fire, you will get burned."

Many of us would never dream of sticking our hand in a fire, knowing the consequences, yet many Christians entertain thoughts of adultery even though they know that every affair on the planet has blown families apart. Solomon states that for the man who commits adultery "his shame will never be wiped away" (Prov. 6:33, NIV). God will forgive any sinner who humbly repents, but humans are not so forgiving. Gifted men with glittering ministries have been discarded in a moment because of adultery. Sports stars have turned from heroes to scumbags and even family friends are judged silently by society for years after the act.

If you're contemplating an affair, remember: if you commit this act you will have the words "adulterer" tattooed on your head for life. I know men in their late seventies who cheated on their wives decades ago, but are still ostracized and made the butt of every joke. I often cite King David as a glorious picture of God's grace for the adulterer because I truly believe that when we mess up, if we confess ours sins to God, the blood of Jesus Christ will wash us whiter than snow. On the flip side, however, let's also not forget that three thousand years later we are still talking about David's infidelity, even though God has long forgiven him.

## *Thought 86—Obedient Children*

*As obedient children, not conforming yourselves
to the former lusts, as in your ignorance.*

First Peter 1:14

John Blanchard said, "To pay the price of obedience is to escape the cost of disobedience."[26] Obedience is costly but disobedience is even more expensive. The verse above reminds us that obedience is expected of us. On a daily basis we are called to renounce our lustful desires, no matter how tempting, and submit our will beneath the will of God. That sounds severe, but we were created for obedience, and when we obey our Creator we discover a wonderful fulfilment. This is my wife's favorite hymn:

> Trust and obey,
> For there's no other way
> To be happy in Jesus,
> But to trust and obey.[27]

In our former state we were like a wild dog with no leash. When our flesh lusted, we pursued, we did not deny our cravings of anything they desired. But now we have a new master, we are under new marching orders and what a privilege that this ruined, stray dog now has a home in the palace where the King of Kings and Lord of Lords dwells! One of the most common ways I like to end my private prayers is like this 'Lord, help me to remember that holiness equals happiness.' Why do I repeat this so often? Because in this lust-saturated culture it's so easy to forget that my greatest source of happiness is to obey the Savior who loved me enough to lay down His precious life for me.

## Thought 87—Thou Shalt Not Covet!

*Where do wars and fights come from among you? Do they not come from your desires for pleasure that war in your members? You lust and do not have. You murder and covet and cannot obtain. You fight and war. Yet you do not have because you do not ask.*

James 4:1–2

I think we've all coveted or lusted after something that doesn't belong to us at some point in our lives. I'm not talking about a normal, healthy desire for a good thing, such as serving in the church in a particular role, or more money to provide for our family, or a larger ministry to reach more souls for Jesus.

But often desires can become impure lusts. We may covet our neighbor's wife, their lifestyle, their popularity. The root of jealousy starts when we believe that what this person has should instead belong to us, and when this happens we've already begun to sin. Love is patient; lust is impatient. Love wants to give; lust wants to get.

Here's the crazy thing: as James points out, when we lust, becoming obsessed with something that isn't ours, it makes us miserable. If I may use a silly example, I remember in my early twenties literally crying in front of the mirror because I was beginning to lose my hair. The more I stared at my receding hairline, the more I looked at my friends who had full heads of hair, the more I was in turmoil. The day I accepted my hairline had been "raptured" was the day I was free from this strife! So accept your lot in life; don't grumble if you don't have a six-figure salary or a beautiful spouse, but rejoice that your name is written in in the Book of Life. After all, Teddy Roosevelt was right when he said, "Comparison is the thief of joy."[28]

## Thought 88—The Transparent Apostle

*For what I am doing, I do not understand. For what I will to do, that I do not practice; but what I hate, that I do.*

Romans 7:15

Paul's transparency in the verse above has comforted many believers over the centuries. First, we realize that even apostles mess up! All the knowledge, all the theology, all the experience does not stop us from failing our Savior and doing things we hate to do.

Second, it shows us that the true believer battles against sin. It's easy for us to doubt our salvation and Christ's love for us when we fall into sexual sin. But the fact that our sin disturbs us and we hate how powerless we are against temptation is a sign that we are in the Lord's army. Most unbelievers don't battle against pornography; they don't feel guilty when their eyes wander. The lost man or woman isn't concerned with pleasing the Lord, because they do not have the Holy Spirit to convict them of sin. When Manchester loses a soccer game, I don't grieve over the loss, because I'm not a Manchester fan. Likewise, the non-Christian feels no sense of guilt when they sin, because they are not on "Team Jesus."

I've heard that Jacksonville Zoo once had a two-headed lizard. The animal caused quite a stir, because often one head wanted to go one direction, and the other head wanted to go another. The poor lizard's legs didn't know which way to turn! That's how it feels to be a Christian at times. One side of us wants to obey Jesus, but the other wants to indulge the flesh. May we get on our knees daily and ask God to deliver us from this double-mindedness and to walk by the Spirit.

## Thought 89—You Won't Explode!

*No temptation has overtaken you except such as is common to man; but God is faithful, who will not allow you to be tempted beyond what you are able.*

First Corinthians 10:13

I remember in my early days as a young Christian, I went to a youth conference. One of the conference teachers said something rather simple, but also rather powerful: "If you resist sexual temptation, you won't burst; you won't explode." How could he say that? Because our faithful God allows only so much tempting bait to be dangled in front of us. God knows you better than you know yourself. We may sometimes wish God did not have so much faith in our strength to resist sin, but He is never wrong.

A friend said to me recently after changing jobs, "I'm now in vulnerable situations where I'm in houses alone with women, and I don't know how I'd react if they threw themselves on me." Praise God that the Lord does know how you'd react—that's why very few Christians find themselves in that position, because sadly many of us would crumble. I have another friend who did find himself in that position, but was amazed at how, in that moment, God gave him the grace to resist.

The Devil tries to isolate us and make us believe our sin is peculiar, that no one understands—but God understands. Our loving Father will not put us in the ring with a super-heavyweight if He knows we are a spiritual featherweight. On the other hand, He will not put us in the ring with a featherweight if He knows we are a spirtual heavyweight. Be prepared to fight some big opponents if the Lord considers us worthy as we live for Him on this earth.

# Thought 90—Solomon's Window Lattice

*For at the window of my house I looked through my lattice,*
*And saw among the simple, I perceived among the youths,*
*A young man devoid of understanding,*

Proverbs 7:6–7

It's amazing what God allows us to see by total accident. Here Solomon doesn't appear to be openly spying, but casually gazing out through the casement of his window, when he sees a young man lacking in common sense, walking to the house of an adulterous woman. I think we've all seen people's eyes wander, and it shocks us because we realize how wicked it looks to others. Ask any woman and she will tell you how uncomfortable it can be when "I can feel his eyes on me." Many a young person has been caught by their parents watching pornography when they least expected it. Many a husband has been caught by his wife lusting after another woman. I even know tragic stories of people who have caught their spouse in bed with someone else. Hagar rightly said, "You are the God who sees me" (Gen. 16:13, NIV).

Let the fact that our sin never goes unnoticed thrust a godly fear in our hearts. You never know who might be watching you when you're watching others. Even if you're smarter than everyone else and never get caught, do you think you will escape God, when you stand before Him at the judgment seat of Christ?

## Thought 91—Radically Change Your Routine

*Passing along the street near her corner; And he took the path to her house In the twilight, in the evening, In the black and dark night.*

Proverbs 7:8–9

Here we find a young man in a place he shouldn't be, at a time he shouldn't be out on the street. "In the black and dark night" literally means "in the center of night, even darkness." The young man is not in the center of light, but darkness.

In the Bible darkness is a picture of men's sin. Nicodemus visited Jesus by night. Why was that specific detail included by the Gospel writer? Because Nicodemus still wanted to remain in the shadows; he wasn't ready to claim the Light of the World publicly. Jesus said that those who loved darkness more than light did so because their deeds were evil (see John 3:19). Many of the lustful sins of this world cannot be committed in the light, for it would expose their shameful wickedness. Unrepentant people refuse to leave their sin behind, which means they have to spend a lot of time in the darkness, late at night, nurturing that sin.

What does your nighttime routine look like? A very practical way to quit any addiction is to radically change the rut you've been living in for years and to transform your routine. If you stay up late watching things you shouldn't, would you be willing to go to bed earlier and rise earlier, as a way of disrupting these sinful habits? The average pornography addict wastes ten hours a week watching wrong images on the Internet. Imagine if you took those ten hours from late at night and converted them into ten productive hours in the morning—you could start a new project, read a Christian book, go to the gym. I guess what I'm really asking you is, don't you think it's finally time for us to become children of the light?

## *Thought 92—The Lady of the Lake*

*But if you do not do so, then take note, you have sinned against the LORD; and be sure your sin will find you out.*

Numbers 32:23

My favorite lake in England is also the deepest—it's called Wast Water. This lake holds a grizzly secret which taints its rugged beauty.

Peter Hogg, a pilot, married a flight attendant named Margaret, nineteen years his junior. The marriage quickly turned sour and Margaret began a stubborn affair with an American banker, refusing to end the relationship. One night a fight broke out between the couple, and Peter killed Margaret. Trying to cover his tracks, Peter wrapped his wife's body in a carpet, drove hundreds of miles north to Wast Water, tied her feet to a concrete block and dumped her body in the middle of the lake. Nine years later, scuba divers noticed something strange. On further inspection, they were horrified to find a face—perfectly preserved like wax in the icy cold waters.

Peter Hogg was caught because he made two fatal mistakes. First, if he had paddled out just ten yards further, the body would have sunk to the bottom, 260 feet deep, beyond the divers' normal limit. Instead, Margaret's body got wedged onto a ridge. Second, Peter forgot to remove Margaret's wedding ring, which had the inscription, "P.H. M.H. 1963." Once this piece of evidence was unraveled, it became very clear who this "lady of the lake" was.[29]

I'm sure you have never committed murder and hidden the body, but we all have secrets we think no one knows about. Peter Hogg is a stark reminder that the Bible does not lie when it says, "Be sure your sin will find you out." Today you have an opportunity to repent and get out from under your sin, practically unscathed. But if you do not take this window of grace, be warned: your sin may expose your secret to the rest of the world.

### *Thought 93—The Most Humbling Verse in the Bible*

*"Fear not, you worm Jacob, You men of Israel! I will help you,"*
*says the LORD And your Redeemer, the Holy One of Israel.*

Isaiah 41:14

A quiz on the Internet asks, "What animal are you?" What would you choose? A strong bear? A loyal dog? A brave lion? A cute dolphin? The choice for many of us may reflect the over-inflated view we have of ourselves. But how does God see us?

In the verse above, we see God speaking gently, not harshly, to the people of Israel, but He refers to them as a worm. That's how insignificant and weak people are compared to the living God. Like a worm on a path on a sunny day, so vulnerable, so easily trodden on. You may feel like that worm, so weak in the battle against lust. But the beautiful truth of the Bible is that Jesus Christ, the Son of God, loved us enough to die on the cross to redeem "worms" like you and me.

The word "worm" in Isaiah can also be translated "scarlet material." Coincidentally, there is a creature called the scarlet (or crimson) worm. This particular worm is unique because when it gives birth it ties its tail to a tree, lays its eggs, and dies. As it dies, it secretes a crimson dye that stains the wood a bright red. The color produced by this worm is so vibrant it was once used as a dye for clothing.[30]

This reminds us of Christ, who was willing to be trodden on for our sin, who, just like the crimson worm, stained the wood of the cross scarlet, dying to give us life. The great God of the universe was willing to be treated no better than a worm, so that He might redeem you. The least we can do in return is seek to serve Him obediently each day.

## *Thought 94—When People Are Exalted*

*So I came out to meet you, Diligently to
seek your face, And I have found you.*

Proverbs 7:15

Three times in this short verse the adulterous woman makes this young man feel special. First, she came out especially to him—out of all the men in the world she longed to meet him. Second, she was diligently looking for his face in the crowd—she didn't want to see any other face but his. Third, she found him—like a precious piece of jewelry she had once lost, now she has found him. Wouldn't such words make anyone feel special?

This tactic isn't used only on men; I've often heard women proudly say about their partner, "He worships the ground I walk on." Manipulative men know that the way to exploit a woman is to make her feel loved, and dumping her once they get what they want.

Why are we so susceptible to flattery? The answer is *pride*. In our flesh, whether we see it or not, is a desire to be exalted, to be admired. The very sin that cast God's most beautiful angel, Lucifer, from heaven is the same sin that would have us desire to be worshipped by others. May we humble ourselves and consider the Savior, who made Himself nothing. He was the one who should be rightfully exalted and worshipped, but He became a servant—to die for our pride, lust, and every other sin. May the thought of Christ and His genuine, sincere love for us be enough that we would not be deceived into seeking love from the wrong places.

## Thought 95—Godly Sorrow Versus Worldly Sorrow

*For godly sorrow produces repentance leading to salvation, not to be regretted; but the sorrow of the world produces death.*

Second Corinthians 7:10

In Psalm 51 David says, "The sacrifices of God are a broken spirit, A broken and a contrite heart—These, O God, You will not despise" (51:17). Why does he say that? Because God wants us to mourn over our sins. There is a brokenness, a godly sorrow, that the Lord will not shun; it will move His heart to have compassion on us. But what is the difference between godly sorrow and worldly sorrow? Godly sorrow leads to action, to the transforming power of the Holy Spirit, who changes us and enables us to turn away from our wickedness. But sadly, I believe many of us are trapped in the wrong kind of sorrow—worldly sorrow. Worldly sorrow is all about self. Suppose a Christian man battling a pornography addiction falls on Saturday, and on Sunday begins to feel resentment. Angry that he wasted the evening, he feels self-pity and mutters words to himself like, "I'm so pathetic; I deserve hell." They feel helplessness, guilt, shame—and if they get caught in this cycle, it leads to depression.

You may ask, "How can you be so diagnostic, Joe?" I think you know why! The day I stopped looking at myself and looked to Christ was the day victory became attainable. New schedules, accountability partners, and sermons definitely helped. But until my love for Christ outgrew my love for myself, I wasn't ready to repent. Let our sorrow be founded not upon self-centeredness but on realizing that Jesus suffered tremendously on the cross for our sin.

# Thought 96—Pampering Pleasure

*I have spread my bed with tapestry, Colored coverings of Egyptian linen. I have perfumed my bed With myrrh, aloes, and cinnamon.*

Proverbs 7:16–17

A friend of mine once said to me, "The problem with sin is that it's so pleasurable." The Bible does not hide this; here in the above two verses Solomon describes the enticement to sexual sin. This adulterous hostess has prepared a luxurious room for the two immoral lovers to enjoy. You can see the exotic artistry and smell the foreign aromas that engage all the senses. Our world is full of this today, this deception that sexual sin is a rich lifestyle, that immorality is "high living," and that those who are not promiscuous are boringly irrelevant in our culture. We see this in advertising, in the shopping malls, and on social media: the life of lust is portrayed as unending luxury and elegance. Note again how the hostess in this verse captures the imagination, making this forbidden fruit an exciting experience that draws the sinner into a vortex of lust.

Pornography has transformed from still images in magazines to video, with every kind of fetish for every kind of perversity. Do not be deceived by the illusion of luxury; the same Solomon warned us that those who love pleasure will be poor. Yes, there are exceptions to the rule, but if you look at the vast majority of those who indulge their carnal desires, they are the same people who walk a difficult road. Even if they are rich materially, they are poor spiritually—and I know which treasure I would prefer!

The sinner who is submerged in the filth of sexual sin should be no more content in it than a man would be content while submerged in a sewer. Any sane person would scream, "Pull me out of this filth!" My prayer for you is that you would see through the mirage of luxury and be repulsed by all sexual sin.

## Thought 97—A City without Walls

*Whoever has no rule over his own spirit*
*Is like a city broken down, without walls.*

Proverbs 25:28

When I was younger I remember reading my Bible early in the morning while on a missions trip, when I came across this verse. The only other person in the room was the team leader, who also happened to be a very good friend. So I asked him what it meant to be "a city without walls." He replied, "It means you can be easily conquered."

A high wall in biblical times was a city's greatest defense; without it, the city was vulnerable to attack. Lack of self-control also leaves us vulnerable to serious attacks from the Enemy. In one hour of rioting a city can lose its economy; in one hour of indiscipline, everything you have worked for in the Lord can be lost—your purity, your victorious streak, your joy, your peace, your reputation. Let's build the walls higher! I'd sooner have an overambitious wall and be seen as "paranoid" than trust in my old garden fence. Never be ashamed to have accountability software on your devices, to always have your door open, to share your phone with your spouse, and to never trust yourself alone with someone you are attracted to. Some probably said the Great Wall of China was excessive when it was built, but it still stands today.

## Thought 98—Sin Turns Men into Mice

*For she has cast down many wounded,*
*And all who were slain by her were strong men.*

Proverbs 7:26

Samson had the strength to kill a thousand Philistine warriors with the jawbone of a donkey, to tear a lion apart like it was a wet paper bag, to bring down a colossal temple with his bare hands—and yet he did not have the power to resist the advances of Delilah. David killed the towering giant Goliath; in battle he conquered his tens of thousands. In fact, he never lost a battle in his life—except the battle of lust. Every year we hear of sports stars who for years had the discipline to rise at 5 a.m. and hustle to the basketball court or football field to train, yet they did not have the self-control to keep their marriage bed pure. We hear of politicians whose election campaigns were imaginative, who had brilliant solutions to world problems and strategic plans to run the country, but could not find a solution to overcome their pornography addiction. We even hear of preachers who were fearless, who could handle the pressure of leading a huge church, who stood in front of thousands and communicated powerfully, but could not handle their temptations.

Lust has slain many, many strong men and women. Do not underestimate your Enemy; you will regret it. There is, however, one strong man who has never been cast down by lust—Jesus Christ. The Lord Jesus kept Himself pure to the very end and that's why you and I would be very wise to hide behind Him. He slayed lust, sin, death, and Satan on the cross—and when you have the Strongest on your side you need not fear any foe.

## Thought 99—It's Decision Time

*But he does not know that the dead are there,*
*That her guests are in the depths of hell.*

Proverbs 9:18

As I draw this book to a close, I feel very conflicted. I don't want to take away from all the promises of grace that we've looked at earlier, but I also want to warn you about the seriousness of impurity. I want to finish on a positive note, but I also don't want to say "peace, peace" when there is no peace. So let me say this: I have been very challenged by the many Bible verses that link unrepentant sexual sin with eternal separation from God (see 1 Cor. 6:9, Rev. 22:14–15, Prov. 7:27, Eph. 5:5, Mark 9:47).

If today your heart is soft towards the Word of God, flee these youthful lusts that have held onto you for so long. Next year there is no guarantee that you will feel the same desire for repentance. That's why you would be very wise to turn from it today. If you've read this book and continued to return to the place where you shouldn't, I plead with you to consider these severe warnings. God is longsuffering and abounding in grace, but He is also a just judge who commands all men everywhere to repent. There will be mistakes on the way, and we will never be the saint we should be this side of eternity—but I'm begging you, as you close this book for the last time, to remember it's not OK to hold the Devil's hand and Christ's at the same time. When you came to Christ He loosed the bonds of your sin. Whom the Son sets free is free indeed! So when we return to sin, we do so willfully—no one forces us and you need to make a decision. Will you obey the Lord's voice and come out of Babylon, or are you quite contented remaining in the city of destruction?

## *Thought 100—A Tremendous Responsibility*

*Keep your heart with all diligence,*
*For out of it spring the issues of life.*

Proverbs 4:23

The way I proposed to my wife was a little weird. I bought a hard-shelled clam from a local fish market, and after scooping the guts out, I taped the engagement ring to the inside and sealed the clam with string. The day I proposed was my wife's birthday. It was a scorching hot day and the plan was I would take Emma "river snorkeling" and drop the clam on the riverbed for her to discover herself.

Except things didn't go according to plan.

My then-girlfriend was angry because I hadn't bought her a birthday present or even a card. So instead of holding my hand while we swam together in a delightful watery plunge pool, she sat on a rock, sulking. Eventually, I gave up trying to convince her to join me and got out of the water exclaiming, "Look what I've found, Emma!" But it was too late; she wasn't speaking to me and wouldn't even turn around!

After five minutes of pleading and desperation, I blurted out, "Emma Davies, for once in your life, do as I say!" There I was on one knee with the open clam in my hand. One half had the ring taped to it and the other half read, "Emma Davies, will you marry me?"

The reason I used a clam is because Emma's golden ring needed to be securely guarded. Everything in this life that is precious is protected. Diamonds are covered by layers of rock, the Crown Jewels in London are patrolled by armed guards, and even your smartphone has a protective case. So why do we not take more diligence to guard something even more valuable—our hearts? That's really been the message of this book: your heart belongs to Jesus, and if He was willing to die for us, the least we can do is to try to keep ourselves pure until He returns.

# References

1. D. Martyn Lloyd-Jones, *Faith on Trial: Psalm 73* (Ross-shire, Scotland: Christian Heritage, 1956).

2. Leonard Ravenhill, *Sodom Had No Bible* (Christian Life Books, 2007).

3. Charles Spurgeon, *Metropolitan Tabernacle Pulpit*, Vol. 32 (Carlisle, PA: Banner of Truth, 1969).

4. Charles Wesley, "Jesus, Lover of my Soul" (hymn), 1740, public domain.

5. J.N. Lenker, *Luther's Catechetical Writings* (Minneapolis: The Luther Press, 1907.

6. Origin unknown. As told to Tèmakamoxkomëhèt by his friend Asuwibi'oxkwe. 'Which One Do You Feed?', Blog Post, N.D, Native American Embassy, accessed April 22, 2020, https://www.nativeamericanembassy.net/www.lenni-lenape.com/www/html/LenapeArchives/LenapeSet-01/feedwich.html.

7. Tryon Edwards, C.N. Catrevas, Jonathan Edwards, *The New Dictionary of Thoughts* (n.c.: Ravenio Books, 2015).

8.  Charles Spurgeon, *New Park Street Pulpit*, 1858, Vol. 4 (Grand Rapids: Baker Books, 1990).

9.  Kelly M. Kapic and Justin Taylor, eds., *Overcoming Sin and Temptation: Three Classic Works by John Owen* (Wheaton, IL: Crossway, 2015).

10. Joseph Castro, "11 Surprising Facts About the Circulatory System," *Live Science* (Future US Inc,), September 25, 2013. https://www.livescience.com/39925-circulatory-system-facts-surprising.html.

11. E.M. Bounds, *Power Through Prayer* (London: Marshall Brothers, 1920).

12. "Marathon man Akhwari demonstrates superhuman spirit" (article), International Olympic Committee, October 18, 1968. https://olympics.com/en/news/marathon-man-akhwari-demonstrates-superhuman-spirit.

13. Tom Leonard, "Lonely twilight of Jack Nicolson as he pays the price for treating women like dirt and now rarely ventures out to his old Hollywood stomping ground" (article), *DailyMail.com* Associated Newspapers Ltd., January 17, 2015. https://www.dailymail.co.uk/tvshowbiz/article-2913870/Jack-Nicholson-pays-lonely-price-treating-women-like-dirt.html.

14. J.C. Ryle, *The Christian Leaders of the Last Century* (Carlisle, PA: Banner of Truth, 1978).

15. Oswald J. Smith, *The Man God Uses* (London: Marshall, Morgan & Scott, 1965).

16. Matthew Henry, *Matthew Henry's Commentary on the Whole Bible: Complete and Unabridged in 6 Volumes* (Hendrickson Publishers, 1991).

17. R.T. Kendall, "Will The Dove Remain?" (article), *Inspiration Ministries*, 2014, accessed May 19, 2019. https://inspiration. org/christian-articles/will-the-dove-remain/

18. C. Bridge, A. McGrath, and J.I. Packer, *Proverbs* (Wheaton, IL: Crossway, 2001).

19. D.L. Moody, *The Overcoming Life: Updated Edition* (Abbotsford, WI: Life Sentence Publishing, 2016).

20. D.L. Moody, *Notes From My Bible: From Genesis To Revelation* (Grand Rapids: Baker Books, 1979).

21. A. Wilkinson, "Successful bank robbers probably earn LESS money than you do" (article), *Mirror/ Reach plc*, March 3, 2015. https://www.mirror.co.uk/news/ampp3d/successful-bank-robbers-probably-earn-5264179.

22. J.R.R. Tolkien, *The Two Towers* (New York: HarperCollins, 2011).

23. Warren Wiersbe, *The Wiersbe Study Bible* (Nashville: Thomas Nelson, 2009).

24. Warren Wiersbe, *Ephesians Through Revelation* (Colorado Springs: David C. Cook, 1992).

25. William Gurnall, *The Christian in Complete Armour* (Peabody, MA: Hendrickson Publishers, 2010).

26. John Blanchard, *The Complete Gathered Gold: A Treasury of Quotations for Christians* (Darlington, UK: Evangelical Press, 2007).

27. J.H. Sammis, "Trust and Obey" (hymn), 1887, public domain.

28. Blanchard.

29. Irving, A. "The lady in the lake" (article), *Whitehaven News* (Newsquest Media Group Ltd,), March 19, 2009. https://www.whitehavennews.co.uk/news/17151162.the-lady-in-the-lake/

30. Larry and Marilyn Johnson, "The Crimson or Scarlet Worm," *Kids Think and Believe, Too* (Alpha Omega Institute), November 2011, https://www.discovercreation.org/documents/kids/KTBNovember-December2011.pdf

**PUBLICATIONS**

Fort Washington, PA 19034

This book is published by CLC Publications, an outreach of CLC Ministries International. The purpose of CLC is to make evangelical Christian literature available to all nations so that people may come to faith and maturity in the Lord Jesus Christ. We hope this book has been life changing and has enriched your walk with God through the work of the Holy Spirit. If you would like to know more about LC, we invite you to visit our website:

**www.clcusa.org**

To know more about the remarkable story of the founding of
CLC International, we encourage you to read

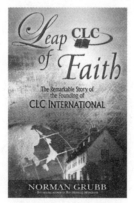

## LEAP OF FAITH

*Norman Grubb*
Paperback
Size 5¹/₄ x 8, Pages 248
ISBN: 978-0-87508-650-7
ISBN (*e-book*): 978-1-61958-055-8

## The Normal Christian Life

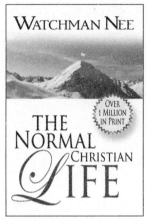

. . . is Watchman Nee's great Christian classic unfolding the central theme of "Christ our Life." Nee reveals the secret of spiritual strength and vitality that should be the normal experience of every Christian.

*Trade paper ISBN: 978-0-87508-990-4*

## The Normal Christian Life Study Guide

Gives a brief summary of each chapter of the book and then gives questions designed to provoke thought and possible discussion.

*Trade paper ISBN: 978-1-61958-129-6*

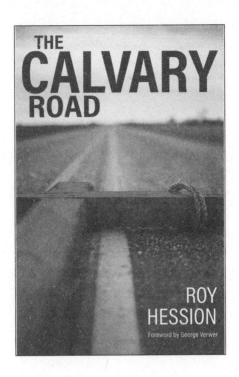

## THE CALVARY ROAD

*Roy Hession*

Do you long for revival and power in your life? Learn how Jesus can fill you with His spirit through brokenness, repentance and confession in this updated version of Hession's classic, *The Calvary Road*. In the course of eleven chapters, Hession emphasizes the need for personal revival in life with Christ.

Paperback
Size 4¹/₄ x 7, Pages 162
ISBN: 978-1-61958-226-2
ISBN (*e-book*): 978-1-61958-227-9

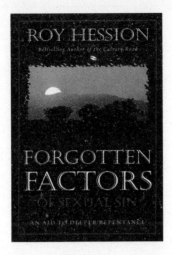

# FORGOTTEN FACTORS
## of Sexual Sin

*Roy Hession*

Pornography, lust, adultery and other sexual sins are rampant in our society, and have even become a problem for many believers.

Why does the church seem to falter so often in ministering to those caught in sexual sin? And why does victory over these sins seem to be so elusive?

Could it be that there are factors in the issues of sexual sin that we have simply forgotten to account for? Could it be that there are deeper issues involved here?

Join Roy Hession as he uncovers these factors and guides the faltering believer to a place of deeper repentance and full freedom from sin.

Paperback
Size 5¹/₄ x 8, Pages 112
ISBN: 978-0-87508-823-5
ISBN (*e-book*): 978-1-61958-112-8